QUESTION BANK IN PLANT SCIENCES

NEW INDIA PUBLISHING AGENCY
New Delhi 110 034

About the Authors

Dr. Akshay I. Patel did his B.Sc. (Agri.) and M.Sc. (Agri.) in Genetics and Plant Breeding from N.M. College of Agriculture, Gujarat Agricultural University, Sardar krushinagar (Gujarat) in the year 1996 and 1999, respectively. He obtained Ph.D. degree in Genetics and Plant Breeding from Navsari Agricultural University, Navsari (Gujarat) in 2008 with first class. Presently, he is working as an Assistant Professor (GPB) ASPEE College of Horticulture & Forestry, Navsari Agricultural University, Navsari. Besides, he is actively involved in teaching and research in the field of vegetable improvement. He has more than 75 research publications in International as well as National journals and 20 popular articles in vernacular language for the benefit of farmers of Gujarat. He also contributed in the development of high yielding varieties of vegetable, flower as well as field crops.

So far he has guided 13 M. Sc. and 3 Ph.D. students in the discipline of Vegetable Science and Genetics and Plant Breeding.

Prof. Kirti Bardhan is currently serving as an assistant professor at the Navsari Agricultural University is able to inspire the next generation. He has taught to Bachelor of Horticulture, Bachelor of Forestry and postgraduate faculty of horticulture and agriculture students and improving their engagement in different aspects of plant biology by the use of blended and active learning pedagogy. For over eight years, he has published more than 30 research articles and guided three master students as a major advisor. He has also qualified ICAR NET in Crop Physiology.

Dr. Vipulkumar B. Parekh is working as Assistant Professor (Biotechnology) at ASPEE College of Horticulture and Forestry, Navsari Agricultural University, Navsari, Gujarat (India). He did Bachelor of Science (Agriculture) from Navsari Agricultural University, Navsari (Gujarat) in 2005 with "Vice chancellors gold medal", Master of Science (Agril. Biotechnology) in 2008, PG Diploma (Agricultural Information Technology) in 2009 from Anand Agricultural University, Anand (Gujarat). He has completed his Ph. D (Plant Molecular Biology and Biotechnology) in 2017 from Navsari Agricultural University, Navsari (Gujarat). Cleared ICAR NET (Agricultural Biotechnology), in 2009. He has published 3 books and about 22 research papers in various national and international repute journals. He is also handling various research projects related plant biotechnology.

Dr. Bimal S. Desai is recruited as Assistant Professor (Botany) at ASPEE College of Horticulture and Forestry, Navsari Agricultural University, Navsari, Gujarat since 2010. He obtained his Bachelors (1996) and Masters degree (1998) in Botany from The M. S. University of Baroda, Gujarat securing first class. Worked with Gujarat Ecology Commission and Gujarat Ecology Society on Biodiversity of Gujarat (1998-2002). Obtained doctoral degree in 2004 in Botany (Ethnobotany and Taxonomy) from The M. S. University of Baroda. He has to his credit 72 research publications, 03 books and 22 popular articles in vernacular language for the benefit of farmers. He has completed two projects sponsored by Gujarat Council of Science and Technology (GUJCOST) and Gujarat Forestry Research Institute (GFRI). His area of specialization is Biodiversity, Taxonomy and Medicinal and Aromatic Plants. He has guided 09 M. Sc. Students on various aspects of Medicinal plants.

QUESTION BANK IN PLANT SCIENCES

Akshay I. Patel
Assistant Professor, Plant Genetics and Breeding
ASPEE College of Horticulture and Forestry
Navsari Agricultural University
Navsari-396 450, Gujarat

Kirti Bardhan
Assistant Professor, Crop Physiology
ASPEE College of Horticulture and Forestry
Navsari Agricultural University
Navsari-396 450, Gujarat

Vipulkumar B. Parekh
Assistant Professor, Crop Biotechnology
ASPEE College of Horticulture and Forestry
Navsari Agricultural University
Navsari-396 450, Gujarat

Bimal S. Desai
Assistant Professor, Botany
ASPEE College of Horticulture and Forestry
Navsari Agricultural University
Navsari-396 450, Gujarat

NEW INDIA PUBLISHING AGENCY
New Delhi 110 034

NEW INDIA PUBLISHING AGENCY

101, Vikas Surya Plaza, CU Block, LSC Market
Pitam Pura, New Delhi 110 034, India
Phone: + 91 (11)27 34 17 17 Fax: + 91(11) 27 34 16 16
Email: info@nipabooks.com
Web: www.nipabooks.com

Feedback at feedbacks@nipabooks.com

ISBN 978-93-89571-13-4

Composed and Designed by NIPA

Prof. Minoo H. Parabia. (FES, FIAAT)

Retd. Prof. & Head, Department of Biosciences
Former Dean, Faculty of Science
Veer Narmad South Gujarat University, Surat, Gujarat
Member, Gujarat Medicinal Plant Board, Gujarat
Surat, Gujarat

Foreword

Study and the evaluation are the parts of education system. Institutions use different methods of evaluation. One of the most widely accepted systems of examinations is to use Objective Questions or Questions with multiple choices (MCQs) as an answers and the examinee has to select one of the choices given as a correct answer. MCQs preparation requires quite a labour on the part of paper setters. Of course, it is easiest for the examiner checking the answers and many times, it does not even require an examiner. A computer with a programme can do the job for us.

The team of young authors have come up with the question bank that can be banked upon by the students and examiners of the University.

Basically it deals with the subjects of biology taught at the Agricultural University.

The coverage is good and the authors have apparently put up great labour to make it as sound as possible. I had an opportunity to leaf through the work and was happy to see the wideness.

Wherever, numerals are involved as an answer, I request the authors and the subsequent users to be careful, unless the answer is bare truth like sixty seconds per minute or twenty four hours in a day. Overlapping or variable number containing questions must be avoided.

In addition to the memory recall the application oriented questions enhance the value of question bank. This is the good beginning and I hope the authors will continue to update this. Good questions force the students to study well and to study in depth.

If I recall, somebody expressed the view, “what if the students read out all the questions before hand?’ My answer is “That’s the most ideal situation”. I will congratulate such student.

29/7/19 **Prof. Minoo H. Parabia**. (FES, FIAAT)

Preface

Student's brain does not need a complicated stuff to digest plant sciences. It requires thorough understanding and an open mind attitude to travel across the basics and logic of subject learnt. One can achieve deep insight into matter through organized and well written content. You don't have to take pain or put stress to go through a highly advanced book to study science / biology / plant sciences. What is often a prerequisite is to get correct and accurate information.

This is the one of the simplest book aimed at learning various aspects / disciplines covered under the very broad / plethora of plant sciences facts and figures. The primary objective of this compilation is to help students analyze their knowledge of plants in context to cell biology, biochemistry, biotechnology, genetics, breeding, plant physiology, medicinal and aromatic plants along with botany.

With the vast and enormous explosion of information available in plant sciences and allied disciplines, exam patterns are totally oriented towards multiple choice questions and objective type questions, as it is more reliable, precise and easier.

We hope this book will be useful to UG and PG students and faculties / teachers engaged in learning and teaching multidisciplinary subjects in plant sciences.

Any valuable suggestions, inputs and positive criticism to improve this educational resource are welcome.

Authors

Contents

1

Aromatic Plants

1. Volatile oils are extracted by which of the following methods?

   a) Steam distillation c) Solvent extraction

   b) Expression d) All of these

2. Which of the following solvents are used for extracting volatile oils by solvent extraction method?

   a) Petroleum ether c) Chloroform

   b) Toluene d) All of these

3. Volatile oils can be separated by which of the following solvents in TLC?

   a) Benzene (100 %) c) Benzene:Chloroform (1:1)

   b) Chloroform (100 %) d) None of these

4. Which is the most common spray reagent used to detect the volatile oils in TLC?

   a) Wagner's reagent c) Ethanolic sulphuric acid

   b) Vanillin sulphuric acid d) Both B and C

5. Citral-a, citral-b, geraniol and geraniol acetate are major chemical constituents found in

   a) *Mentha piperita* c) *Cymbopogon flexuosus*

   b) *Citronella java* d) *Ocimum sanctum*

6. The highest geraniol content (75-90 %) is found in which of the following aromatic plant variety?

   a) *Cymbopogon martini* var. *sofia*

   b) *Cymbopogon martini* var. *motia*

c) *Cymbopogon nardus*

d) All of these

7. *Cymbopogon winterianus* is native to

a) India | c) Java
b) Sri Lanka | d) Both B and C

8. Benzyl benzoate, Benzyl alcohol and Benzaldehyde are mainly obtained from whicharomatic plant of the following?

a) *Ocimum sanctum* | c) *Jasminum grandiflorum*
b) *Mentha spicata* | d) *Polianthes tuberosa*

9. How many species of *Mentha* are found in India?

a) 04 | c) 09
b) 06 | d) 02

10. Major chemical compound of spearmint is

a) Menthol | c) Carvone
b) Eugenol | d) Thymol

11. Botanical name of Lemon mint is

a) *Mentha piperita* | c) *Mentha arvensis*
b) *Mentha citrata* | d) *Mentha spicata*

12. The main chemical compounds found in Basil are

a) Linalool | c) Methyl cinnamate
b) Methyl chevicol | d) All of these

13. *Pelargonium graveolens* (Geranium) is native to

a) China | c) South Africa
b) Malaysia | d) West Indies

14. The major chemical constituents of Patchouli are

a) α pyrone | c) β sitosterol
b) β octacosanol | d) All of these

15. *Vetiveria zizanioides* (khas khas) is native to

a) Europe | c) USA
b) India | d) China

16. Simple procedure of using vapour pressure to separate the essential oil components is called as

a) Steam distillation
b) Expression
c) Both A and C
d) Distillation

17. Involving water steam combinations, how many types of distillation methods are used for extraction?

a) 01
b) 03
c) 02
d) 04

18. Which among the following methods is specifically used to extract volatile contents of *Citrus*?

a) Steam distillation
b) Hydro diffusion
c) Expression
d) Destructive distillation

19. Best method to extract Jasmine and Tuberose oil is

a) Expression
b) Destructive distillation
c) Enflourage method
d) Steam distillation

20. Which amongst the following is the best method to extract flowers of Orange and Rose?

a) Enflourage method
b) Maceration or Hot fat extraction
c) Steam distillation
d) Hydro diffusion

21. RRL – 011 is the improved variety of

a) *Ocimum bascilicum*
b) *Ocimum canum*
c) *Ocimum sanctum*
d) *Ocimum tenuiflorum*

22. Terpenes with five carbon atoms is called

a) Monoterpenoids
b) Di Terpenoids
c) Hemiterpenoids
d) Tri Terpenoids

23. Terpenes with infinite carbon atoms is called

a) Poly Terpenoids
b) Tri Terpenoids
c) Di Terpenoids
d) All of these

24. The Cochin oil grass is

a) *Cymbopogon pendula*
c) *Cymbopogon citratus*
b) *Cymbopogon flexuosus*
d) *Cymbopogon khasianum*

25. Which amongst the following is the botanical source of Japanese mint?

a) *Mentha spicata*
c) *Mentha arvensis*
b) *Mentha citrata*
d) *Mentha piperita*

26. Palmarosa grows well with soil pH of

a) 6.0 – 6.5
b) 5.0 – 5.5
b) 5.5 – 6.0
d) 6.5 – 7.0

27. Which one of the following is the highly sophisticated recent technology for extraction of volatile oils?

a) Supercritical fluid extraction
b) High performance thin layer chromatography
c) Gas Chromatography
d) Solvent extraction

28. Which among the following is extensively used in Supercritical fluid extraction?

a) NO_2
c) CO
b) CO_2
d) SO_2

29. Which plant part in *Artemisia pallens*, has maximum oil content?

a) Whole plant
c) Leaves
b) Flowers
d) Branches

30. Pragati, a clonal selection from OD -19 variety of lemon grass was developed by

a) NBRI, Lucknow
c) RRL, Jammu Tawi
b) CDRI, Lucknow
d) CIMAP, Lucknow

31. Which variety of Lemon grass was released exclusively for cultivation in South Indian states?

a) Pragati
c) RRL – 16
b) RRL – 39
d) Kaveri

32. Which part of lemon grass yields highest Citral content?
    a) Only green leaves
    b) Full dry leaves
    c) Whole plant with leaves & flowers
    d) Half dry leaves

33. What is the botanical source of East Indian Geranium oil or Russa oil?
    a) *Cymbopogon martini*
    b) *Cymbopogon martini* var. *motia*
    c) *Cymbopogon martini* var. *sophia*
    d) *Cymbopogon flexousus*

34. What is the botanical source of Ginger grass oil?
    a) *Cymbopogon martini* var. *sophia*
    b) *Cymbopogon flexousus*
    c) *Cymbopogon martini*
    d) *Cymbopogon martini* var. *motia*

35. What is the botanical source of Ceylon *Citronella*?
    a) *Cymbopogon martini*
    b) *Cymbopogon winterianus*
    c) *Cymbopogon nardus*
    d) None of these

36. What is the botanical source of Jawa *Citronella*?
    a) *Cymbopogon martini*
    b) *Cymbopogon winterianus*
    c) *Cymbopogon nardus*
    d) *Cymbopogon flexousus*

37. With respect to quality, oil obtained from Ceylon Citronella is ________ to oil obtained from Jawa Citronella.
    a) Inferior
    b) Superor
    c) Same
    d) None of the above

38. Citral percantage in Citriodora oil obtained from *Eucalyptus citriodora* containsranges from
    a) 70-75 %
    b) 75-80 %
    c) 85-90 %
    d) 90-95 %

39. Which is the major chemical component in Bergamont mint?

a) Eugenol
b) Linalyl acetate
c) Linalool
d) Both B and C

40. Maximum content of menthol, menthyl acetate and menthone is found in

a) Japanese mint
b) Peppermint
c) Spearmint
d) Bergamont mint

41. Which is the largest producer of all the mint varieties?

a) USA
b) India
c) China
d) UK

42. Which species of mint is largely cultivated in Indian sub continent?

a) *Mentha citrata*
b) *Mentha spicata*
c) *Mentha arvensis*
d) *Mentha piperata*

43. Which of the following is the improved variety of Japanense mint?

a) Koshi
b) Gomati (EC - 41911)
c) Himalaya (MAS-1, MAS-2)
d) All of these

44. MSS-1, MSS-5, Arka and Neera are improved varieties of

a) Spearmint
b) Bergamont mint
c) Japanese mint
d) Peppermint

45. The only variety Kukrail, released by CIMAP, Lucknow is the improved variety of

a) Bergamont mint
b) Japanese mint
c) Spearmint
d) Peppermint

46. How many volatile compounds have been identified from *Vanilla planifolia*?

a) 120
b) 170
c) 220
d) 270

47. What is the botanical source of Brandy mint or Black mint?

a) *Mentha piperita*
c) *Mentha citrata*
b) *Mentha spicata*
d) *Mentha arvensis*

48. In India, even though *Ocimum* spp are widely spread, the commercial cultivation is found mainly in

a) Maharashtra and Gujarat
b) Rajasthan and Maharashtra
c) Uttar Pradesh and Madhya Pradesh
d) Gujarat and Madhya Pradesh

49. Which amongst the following is mainly cultivated in India?

a) *Tagetes patula*
c) *Tagetes erecta*
b) *Tagetes minuta*
d) *Tagetes lucida*

50. The principle chemical constituents found in *Tagetes* is

a) Alkaloids
c) Phenols
b) Flavonoids
d) Both B and C

Answer Key

1.	**d**	2.	**d**	3.	**c**	4.	**d**	5.	**c**	6.	**b**	7.	**d**	8.	**c**
9.	**a**	10.	**c**	11.	**b**	12.	**d**	13.	**c**	14.	**d**	15.	**b**	16.	**d**
17.	**b**	18.	**a**	19.	**c**	20.	**a**	21.	**a**	22.	**c**	23.	**a**	24.	**b**
25.	**c**	26.	**d**	27.	**a**	28.	**b**	29.	**b**	30.	**d**	31.	**d**	32.	**c**
33.	**b**	34.	**a**	35.	**b**	36.	**c**	37.	**a**	38.	**c**	39.	**d**	40.	**b**
41.	**a**	42.	**c**	43.	**d**	44.	**a**	45.	**d**	46.	**b**	47.	**a**	48.	**c**
49.	**b**	50.	**d**												

2

Dendrology

1. *Litsea chinensis* belongs to which family of flowering plants?
   a) Apocynaceae c) Lauraceae
   b) Rubiaceae d) Fabaceae
2. Genera plantarum was compiled by
   a) Carl Linneaus c) Hooker
   b) Huxley d) Brandis
3. The Greek meaning of the word Xylem is
   a) Wood c) Xylogenesis
   b) Woody d) Xylon
4. The only branched palm found in India is
   a) *Hyphaene indica* c) *Borassus flabellifer*
   b) *Hyphaene dichotoma* d) Both A and B
5. *Tectona grandis* L.f. Linn. is which type of botanical name?
   a) Valid name c) Binomial name
   b) Non valid name d) Legitimate name
6. The new name for the family Palmae is
   a) Arecaceae c) Araceae
   b) Poaceae d) Fabaceae
7. *Callophyllum inophyllum* is rare and endemic to
   a) Western Ghats c) Western Himalayas
   b) Eastern Ghats d) Eastern Himalayas

8. The new name for family Guttiferae is
   a) Clusiaceae
   b) Moraceae
   c) Alangiaceae
   d) Apocynaceae
9. The collection of shrubs is called
   a) Arboretum
   b) Fruticetum
   c) Viticetum
   d) All of these
10. The oldest collections of xylarium is located at
   a) University of Leningrad
   b) Arnold arboretum
   c) Oxford Forestry Institute Xylarium
   d) USDA Forest Product Laboratory
11. *Diospyros montana* belongs to family
   a) Malvaceae
   b) Asteraceae
   c) Apocynaceae
   d) Ebenaceae
12. *Boswellia serrata* belongs to family
   a) Rutaceae
   b) Menispermaceae
   c) Burseraceae
   d) Meliaceae
13. Species plantarum was compiled by
   a) Hooker
   b) Brandis
   c) Linnaeus
   d) Huxley
14. *Couropita guinensis* is commonly called as
   a) chebulic myrobalan
   b) Indian coral tree
   c) Cannon ball tree
   d) Mast tree
15. *Tectona grandis* belongs to
   a) Apocynaceae
   b) Sterculiaceae
   c) Tiliaceae
   d) Verbenaceae
16. Which of the following is/are the most potential allelochemical compound found in plants
   a) Terpenes
   b) Alkaloids
   c) Phenols
   d) Both a and b

17. The botanical name of Red silk cotton tree is
    a) *Ceiba pentandra* c) *Bombax insgine*
    b) *Bombax ceiba* d) *Bombax mori*

18. The botanical name of Chariot tree is
    a) *Tectona grandis* c) *Cassia renigera*
    b) *Ougeinia oojeinsis* d) *Cassia tora*

19. English common name of *Firmiana colorata* is
    a) Sagwan tree c) Pride of India
    b) Cork tree d) The scarlet sterculia

20. The synonym of *Cassia marginata* is also called as
    a) *Cassia roxburghii* c) *Cassia siamea*
    b) *Cassia occidentalis* d) *Cassia italica*

21. The Flora of British India was written by
    a) Brandis c) Hooker
    b) Bentham d) Huxley

22. Yellow silk cotton tree belongs to
    a) Moraceae c) Apiaceae
    b) Bixaceae d) Cochlospermaceae

23. The botanical name of flame of forest tree is
    a) *Butea monosperma* var. *alba*
    b) *Butea parvilfora*
    c) *Butea monosperma*
    d) *Butea frondosa*

24. Inflorescence in *Tectona grandis* L.f. is
    a) Raceme c) Both of these
    b) Panicle d) Cymose

25. *Tridax procumbens* is weed from ___ region of world
    a) Central America c) Tropical Australia
    b) Tropical Africa d) Galapagos islands

26. Yellow variety of *Butea* is found at ___ forest of Gujarat
    a) Central Gujarat   c) South Gujarat
    b) North Gujarat   d) Both a and b
27. Which is the most invasive species of weed in India
    a) *Parthenium hysterophorus*   c) *Eichornia crassipes*
    b) *Lantana camara*   d) Both a and b
28. Which species of *Cassia* is called Indian Amaltas Tree?
    a) *Cassia javanica*   c) *Cassia fistula*
    b) *Cassia tora*   d) *Cassia marginata*
29. Which species of *Ficus* has lanceolate leaves?
    a) *Ficus longifolia*   c) *Ficus benghalensis*
    b) *Ficus carica*   d) *Ficus racemosa*
30. *Phanera purpurea* belongs to which flowering plant family?
    a) Caesalpiniaceae   c) Rubiaceae
    b) Bignoniaceae   d) Sterculiaceae
31. *Dillenia pentagyna* is ____ tree
    a) Rare   c) Endemic
    b) Common   d) Endangered
32. *Thespesia populnea* is commonly called as
    a) Yellow Bhendi tree   c) Indian kino tree
    b) Indian tulip tree   d) Devil's tree
33. *Terminalia crenulata* is a synonym of
    a) *Terminalia tomentosa*   c) *Terminalia elliptica*
    b) *Terminalia catappa*   d) *Terminalia arjuna*
34. *Hyphaene dichotoma* is called as
    a) Diu tad   c) Branched palm
    b) Ravan tad   d) All of these
35. The most common *Diospyros* species found in Indian Forests is
    a) *Diospyros montana*   c) *Diospyros chloroxylon*
    b) *Diospyros Kaki*   d) *Diospyros Melanoxylon*

36. Flower colour of *Azadirachta indica* is
   a) White   c) Yellowish white
   b) Creamy white   d) Dirty white

37. Flower colour of *Cassia fistula* is
   a) Pink   c) Yellow
   b) Purple   d) Red

38. Flower colour of *Erythrina indica* is
   a) Indigo   c) Red
   b) Blue   d) White

39. Which is the oldest living fossil?
   a) *Ginkgo biloba*   c) *Taxus baccata*
   b) *Macrozamia* spp.   d) *Welwitchia* spp.

40. New name for the family compositae is
   a) Sapindaceae   c) Sapotaceae
   b) Plumbaginaceae   d) Asteraceae

41. New name for the family Labiatae is
   a) Sterculiaceae   c) Lamiaceae
   b) Loganiaceae   d) Rubiaceae

42. New name for the family Graminae is
   a) Poaceae   c) Lythraceae
   b) Tiliaceae   d) Compositae

43. New name for the family Umbelliferae is
   a) Capparidaceae   c) Solanaceae
   b) Cleomaceae   d) Apiaceae

44. Woody plants and climbers of British India was compiled / written by
   a) Santapau   c) Talbott
   b) Hooker   d) Brandis

45. *Careya arborea* belongs to family
   a) Moringaceae   c) Lecythidoaceae
   b) Magnoliaceae   d) Sapotaceae

46. *Rhizophora* and *Avicennia* are examples of
    a) Mangroves c) Xerophytes
    b) Halophytes d) Hydrophytes
47. *Balsamodendron mukul* is the old name of
    a) *Commiphora wightii* c) *Commiphora molmol*
    b) *Commiphora mukul* d) *Commiphora myrhh*
48. Largest unipinnate leaf is found in
    a) *Cassia auriculata* c) *Prosopis juliflora*
    b) *Mangifera indica* d) *Toona ciliata*
49. Largest tripinnate leaf is found in
    a) *Oroxylum indicum* c) *Polyalthia longifolia*
    b) *Sterculia urens* d) None of these
50. Total number of Flowering plant families as described by Bentham and Hooker accounts to
    a) 201 c) 203
    b) 202 d) 204
51. Botanical name of kadaya gum tree is
    a) *Sterculia urens* c) *Sterculia guttata*
    b) *Sterculia foetida* d) *Sterculia villosa*
52. Botanical name of Safed Jamun is
    a) *Sygyzium cumini* c) *Eugenia caryophyllata*
    b) *Sygyzium heyneanum* d) *Sygyzium rubicandum*
53. Botanical name of ratangunj Red Bead tree is (Bead tree)
    a) *Acacia tortilis* c) *Vitex negundo*
    b) *Adenanthera pavonina* d) *Adenanthera foveolata*
54. *Kydia calycina* belongs to
    a) Combretaceae c) Rhamnaceae
    b) Malvaceae d) Asteraceae
55. *Dillenia pentagyna* belongs to
    a) Anacardiaceae c) Dilleniaceae
    b) Sapotaceae d) None of these

56. Botanical name of harde chebulic myrobalans is
    a) *Terminalia arjuna* c) *Terminalia catappa*
    b) *Terminalia bellerica* d) *Terminalia chebula*

57. Botanical name of baheda is Belleric myrobalans
    a) *Terminalia arjuna* c) *Terminalia arjuna*
    b) *Terminalia bellerica* d) *Terminalia bellerica*

58. Flora of Gujarat was written by
    a) G. L. Shah c) M. H. Parabia
    b) B. G. Vashi d) S. D. Sabnis

59. The type genus of family Rubiaceae is
    a) *Morinda citrifolia* c) *Rubia cordifolia*
    b) *Randia dumetorum* d) *Randia uliginosa*

60. Interpetiolar stipules are common morphological feature of which plant family?
    a) Rubiaceae c) Euphorbiaceae
    b) Apocynaceae d) Alangiaceae

61. Marking nut is the common name of
    a) *Tectona grandis* c) *Bridelia retusa*
    b) *Semecarpus anacardium* d) *Bridelia squamosa*

62. Soap nut is the common name of which plant genera?
    a) *Sapindus* c) Alibizia
    b) *Acacia* d) Ficus

63. The *Cinchona* tree belongs to
    a) Magnoliaceae c) Poaceae
    b) Rubiaceae d) Asclepiadaceae

64. *Butea monosperma* var. *lutea* has which flower colour?
    a) Yellow c) Blue
    b) White d) Pink

65. *Anacardium occidentale* has its origin from
    a) Mexico c) Tropical Australia
    b) Tropical America d) Madagascar

66. National Botanical Garden is located at
   a) Mumbai
   b) Bangalore
   c) Kolkatta
   d) Chennai

67. FRI stands for
   a) Food research institute
   b) Fodder research institute
   c) Forest research institute
   d) All of these

68. Blatter herbarium is abbreviated by
   a) BLAT
   b) NHB
   c) NHM
   d) NMPB

69. The study of geographical distribution of plant is called
   a) Zoogeography
   b) Biogeography
   c) Phyto geography
   d) Geography

70. *Cassia occidentalis* is a weed from
   a) South America
   b) Latin America
   c) Tropical Africa
   d) Australia

71. *Bauhinia* with single stamen is
   a) *Bauhinia purpurea*
   b) *Bauhinia foveolata*
   c) *Bauhinia monandra*
   d) *Bauhinia variegata*

72. Tree with maximum number of stamens (250) is
   a) *Bombax ceiba*
   b) *Bombax mori*
   c) *Bombax insigne*
   d) *Ceiba pentandra*

73. Botanical name of Alexandrian laurel is
   a) *Calophyllum inophyllum*
   b) *Sterculia foetida*
   c) *Dillenia indica*
   d) *Achras sapota*

74. Botanical name of African Monkey's bread tree is
   a) *Aegle marmelos*
   b) *Adansonia digitata*
   c) *Anogeissus latifolia*
   d) *Azadirachta indica*

75. Botanical name of sugar apple is
   a) *Annona reticulata*
   b) *Annona muricata*
   c) *Annona squamosa*
   d) None of these

76. Fruits of *Terminalia* is called

a) Mericarps | c) Lomentum
b) Pericarps | d) Capsule

77. Heart shaped leaves are found in

a) *Adina cordifolia* | c) Rubia cordifolia
b) *Haldinia cordifolia* | d) All of these

78. Botanical name of Shallaki or shallai gugal is

a) *Bombax ceiba* | c) *Boswellia serrata*
b) *Bauhinia blakeana* | d) *Butea frondosa*

79. *Litsea chinensis* is endemic to

a) Gujarat | c) Maharashtra
b) Assam | d) Madhya Pradesh

80. *Bixa orellaena* belongs to

a) Liliaceae | c) Lauraceae
b) Rutaceae | d) Bixaceae

81. *Hardwickia binnata* belongs to

a) Mimosaceae | c) Bombacaceae
b) Caesalpiniaceae | d) Alangiaceae

82. Sterile stamens are called

a) Tetradynamous stamens | c) Didynamous stamens
b) Polyadelphous stamens | d) Staminodes

83. *Prosopis juliflora* has its origin from

a) India | c) Australia
b) China | d) Mexico

84. Botanical name of charoli/chironjii/cuddapah Almond is

a) *Buchanania lanzan* | c) *Moringa oleifera*
b) *Juglans regia* | d) *Acacia senegal*

85. Kew botanical garden is located at

a) New York | c) Washington
b) London | d) Berlin

86. Botanical name of Queen of Java is
   a) *Cassia tora* c) *Cassia javanica*
   b) *Cassia marginata* d) *Cassia italica*
87. India's largest herbaria is located at
   a) Dehradun c) Varanasi
   b) Kolkatta d) Solan
88. Botanical name of Pagoda tree is
   a) *Plumeria alba* c) Plumeria rubra
   b) *Plumeria acutifolia* d) Plumeria acuminata
89. English common name of *Thevetia peruviana* is
   a) Red oleander c) White oleander
   b) Pink oleander d) Yellow oleander
90. English common name of *Annona muricata* is
   a) Bengal quino c) Bengal almond
   b) Bullock's heart d) Mast tree
91. Dendrology is study of
   a) Woody shrubs c) Woody climbers
   b) Trees d) All of these
92. Botanical name of Mustard tree is
   a) *Salvadora persica* c) *Santalum album*
   b) *Salvadora oleoides* d) *Sterculia villosa*
93. Botanical name of Golden fig is
   a) *Ficus racemosa* c) *Ficus krishnae*
   b) *Ficus benjamina* d) *Ficus rumphii*
94. Botanical name of Brazilian coral tree is
   a) *Cassia marginata* c) *Cassia auriculata*
   b) *Cassia fistula* d) All of these
95. Trumpet tree belongs to family
   a) Sterculiaceae c) Pinaceae
   b) Bignoniaceae d) Cycadaceae

96. *Taxus baccata* is example of
   a) Angiosperm   c) Phanerogams
   b) Gymnosperm   d) Both a and b

97. Botanical name of Australian peppermint tree is
   a) *Eucalyptus amygdalina*   c) *Eucalyptus torelina*
   b) *Eucalyptus tereticornis*   d) None of these

98. Collection of orchids is called
   a) Orchidarium   c) Pinetum
   b) Herbarium   d) Bambusetum

99. Collection of arborescent species is called
   a) Arboretum   c) Herbal garden
   b) Botanical garden   d) Fruticetum

100. Arnold arboretum has a total area of
   a) 260 acres   C 270 acres
   b) 264 acres   d) 280 acres

Answer Key

1.	**c**	2.	**a**	3.	**a**	4.	**d**	5.	**d**	6.	**a**	7.	**a**	8.	**a**
9.	**b**	10.	**a**	11.	**d**	12.	**c**	13.	**c**	14.	**c**	15.	**d**	16.	**c**
17.	**b**	18.	**b**	19.	**d**	20.	**a**	21.	**c**	22.	**d**	23.	**c**	24.	**c**
25.	**a**	26.	**a**	27.	**d**	28.	**c**	29.	**a**	30.	**a**	31.	**d**	32.	**c**
33.	**a**	34.	**c**	35.	**d**	36.	**c**	37.	**c**	38.	**c**	39.	**b**	40.	**d**
41.	**c**	42.	**a**	43.	**d**	44.	**c**	45.	**c**	46.	**d**	47.	**a**	48.	**d**
49.	**a**	50.	**b**	51.	**a**	52.	**b**	53.	**b**	54.	**b**	55.	**c**	56.	**d**
57.	**d**	58.	**a**	59.	**c**	60.	**a**	61.	**b**	62.	**a**	63.	**b**	64.	**a**
65.	**b**	66.	**c**	67.	**c**	68.	**a**	69.	**c**	70.	**a**	71.	**b**	72.	**c**
73.	**a**	74.	**b**	75.	**c**	76.	**a**	77.	**d**	78.	**c**	79.	**b**	80.	**d**
81.	**b**	82.	**d**	83.	**c**	84.	**a**	85.	**b**	86.	**c**	87.	**b**	88.	**d**
89.	**b**	90.	**b**	91.	**b**	92.	**a**	93.	**b**	94.	**a**	95.	**b**	96.	**b**
97.	**a**	98.	**a**	99.	**a**	100.	**b**								

3

Medicinal and Aromatic Plants

1. How many medicinal plant species are shortlisted for cultivation in Gujarat?
   a) 30 c) 20
   b) 32 d) 22
2. The total number of medicinal plants in Gujarat are
   a) 1315 c) 1312
   b) 1300 d) 1330
3. The total number of licensed pharmacies in Gujarat are
   a) 407 c) 408
   b) 410 d) 409
4. How many herbal drug manufactures follow GMP rules in Gujarat?
   a) 47 c) 49
   b) 48 d) 50
5. How many species of *Curcuma* is found in India?
   a) 04 c) 05
   b) 03 d) 02
6. Artemisin, a potential antimalarial drug is obtained from
   a) *Ocimum sanctum* c) *Artemisia ferox*
   b) *Artemisia annua* d) *Artemisia bipinnata*
7. The botanical name of dudhio vachnag is, Flame lily, Glory lily
   a) *Butea monosperma* c) *Gymnema sylvestre*
   b) *Crinum latifolium* d) *Gloriosa superba*

8. Taxol is obtained from
   a) *Pinus roxburghii* c) *Taxus baccata*
   b) *Taxus wallichiana* d) *Cycas circinalis*
9. The current demand of Shallai gum is
   a) 200 T c) 220 T
   b) 210 T d) 215 T
10. Botanical source of shallai gum is
   a) *Commiphora wightii* c) *Commiphora mukul*
   b) *Boswellia serrata* d) *Commiphora myrrh*
11. According to world bank report, the international herbal medicinal market is expected to reach up to
   a) US $ 5 trillion c) US $ 4 trillion
   b) US $ 3 trillion d) US $ 2 trillion
12. The most ancient work on medicinal plants is
   a) Charak samhita c) Aryabhishek
   b) Sushruta samhita d) All of these
13. Select endangered species from the following
   a) *Melia azaderach* c) *Lochnera rosea*
   b) *Podophyllum hexandrum* d) *Gloriosa superba*
14. How many species of the genus *Bursera* is available in India?
   a) 05 c) 04
   b) 03 d) 02
15. What is the botanical name of Bael?
   a) *Aegle marmelos* c) *Terminalia catappa*
   b) *Azadirachta indica* d) *Alpinia galanga*
16. Botanical name of harde is *Chebulic myrobalans*
   a) *Terminalia arjuna* c) *Terminalia bellerica*
   b) *Terminalia chebula* d) *Terminalia tomentosa*
17. Chebolic myrobalans belongs to which plant family?
   a) Combretaceae c) Asteraceae
   b) Papilionaceae d) Mimosaceae

18. Which of the following is the botanical name of baheda? Belleric myrobalans
    a) *Terminalia arjuna* c) *Terminalia bellerica*
    b) *Terminalia chebula* d) *Terminalia tomentosa*
19. *Curcuma zeodaria* is found commonly in
    a) Gujarat c) Maharashtra
    b) Assam d) Madhya Pradesh
20. What is the botanical name of Haridwar Tulsi?
    a) *Ocimum kilimanjaricum* c) *Ocimum canum*
    b) *Ocimum sanctum* d) *Ocimum bascilicum*
21. What is the botanical name of drug Noni?
    a) *Morinda pubescens* c) *Morinda citrifolia*
    b) *Morinda tomentosa* d) All of these
22. *Costus speciosus* belongs to which plant family?
    a) Apocynaceae c) Rubiaceae
    b) Zingiberaceae d) Rhamnaceae
23. Vincristine and Vinblastine is obtained from
    a) *Catharanthus roseus* c) *Catharanthus pusillus*
    b) *Lochnera rosea* d) All of these
24. Steviosides is obtained from
    a) *Rauwoifia* c) *Stevia*
    b) *Withania* d) *Gloriosa*
25. The botanical name of Indan Liquorice is
    a) *Glycyrrhiza glabra* c) *Abrus precatorius*
    b) *Pongamia pinnata* d) *Solanum trilobatum*
26. Kavanch is the most effective medicine for *Mucuna prurita*
    a) Epilepsy c) Down's syndrome
    b) Parkinson's disease d) Memory loss
27. *Terminalia arjuna* is the best remedy for curing
    a) Urinary infections c) Cardiac diseases
    b) Liver complaints d) Digestive problems

28. The optimum pH for cultivating *Withania somnifera* ranges between

a) 6.0 to 6.5 c) 7.0 to 7.5
b) 6.5 to 7.0 d) 7.5 to 8.0

29. The headquarter of IUCN is located at

a) London c) Berlin
b) Washington DC d) New York

30. Which chemical compound is extracted from *Gloriosa superba*?

a) Volatile oils c) Proteins
b) Sugars d) Colchicines

31. Botanical name of Ashwagandha Indian Ginseng is

a) *Withania coagulans* c) *Penax ginseng*
b) *Withania somnifera* d) Both a and b

32. How many biodiversity hotspots are identified in world?

a) 27 c) 25
b) 24 d) 26

33. How many countries are declared as mega biodiversity countries?

a) 10 c) 11
b) 12 d) 13

34. Which of the following is anticancerous plant?

a) *Taxus baccata* c) *Ginkgo biloba*
b) *Vinca rosea* d) *Digitalis purpurea*

35. *Costus speciosus* is propagated mainly by

a) Bulb c) Rhizomes
b) Tubers d) Both A and B

36. *Aegle marmelos* belongs to Family

a) Meliaceae c) Burseraceae
b) Apocynaceae d) Rutaceae

37. Which is the best method to propagate Bael?

a) Cutting c) Both of these
b) Grafting d) None of these

38. *Caesalpinia sappan* is propagated through
   a) Vegetative means c) Cutting
   b) Seeds d) Grafting
39. The trade name of Harde is
   a) Hirda c) Haritaki
   b) Indian myrobalan d) Sriparni
40. *Costus speciosus* will grow better in
   a) Moist localities c) Moist & shaded
   b) Dry localities d) Sandy localities
41. *Coleus aromaticus* belongs to
   a) Fabaceae c) Bignoniaceae
   b) Asteraceae d) Lamiaceae
42. The current research on *Curcuma longa* has proved that it is the best remedy for
   a) Anticancerous
   c) Antiageing
   b) Ischaemic heart & brain problems
   d) Anthelmintic
43. Which plant parts of *Acorus calamus* is used as medicines?
   a) Roots c) Only roots
   b) Leaves d) Both A & B
44. The trade name of *Acorus calamus* is
   a) Indian ginseng c) Indan sarsaparilla
   b) Sweet Flag d) None of these
45. *Coleus forskohlii* is best propagated by
   a) Seeds c) Cutting of young shoot
   b) Cuttings of old shoots d) Both A & C
46. Which soil type is more suitable for cultivation of *Coleus forskohlii*?
   a) Porous c) Porous reddish soil
   b) Porous sandy loam d) Non porous

47. The nutritive drink prepared from Noni is rich in
    a) Carbohydrates c) Fibres
    b) Proteins d) Micronutrients

48. Trade name of *Alpinia galanga* is
    a) Indian Catarrh Root c) Java Galangal
    b) Greater Galangal d) All of these

49. Which part of *Alpinia galanga* is utilized for medicines?
    a) Wet rhizome c) Both of these
    b) Dried rhizome d) None of these

50. *Alpinia galanga* is native of
    a) India c) Bangladesh
    b) China d) Java

51. Which is the most potential contaminant that spoils medicinal plants?
    a) Mercuric chloride c) Sulphuric acid
    b) Aflatoxin d) Nitric acid

52. How many new plant based drugs has been discovered between 2000 to 2005?
    a) 23 c) 24
    b) 22 d) 25

53. Which country has the largest market for herbal products in North America?
    a) California c) Mexico
    b) Barcelona d) USA

54. Which of the following has huge market potential now a days?
    a) Cosmetics c) Nuetraceuticals
    b) Pharmaceuticals d) All of these

55. Trade name of Ashwagandha is
    a) Indian ginseng c) Indian sarsaparilla
    b) Indian periwinkle d) Indian Bedellium

56. English common name of *Vinca rosea* is

a) Spanish periwinkle c) Indian periwinkle

b) Holy basil d) St. John's wart

57. *Alpinia officinarum* is native of

a) Northern China c) Asia

b) Southern China d) Madagascar

58. Curcuminoids extracted from *Curcuma* spp. belongs to which class of chemical compounds?

a) Phenols c) Tannins

b) Alkaloids d) Terpenes

59. Which amongst the following has longer rhizome length?

a) *Curcuma zeodaria* c) *Curcuma aromatica*

b) *Curcuma longa* d) *Curcuma amada*

60. Which of the following species of *Ocimum* yields camphor?

a) *Ocimum canum* c) *Ocimum basilicum*

b) *Ocimum americanum* d) *Ocimum tenuiflorum*

61. National Botanical Research Institute is located at

a) Delhi c) Mumbai

b) Chennai d) Lucknow

62. Central Institute of Medicinal and Aromatic Plants is abbreviated as

a) CIMAP c) CMIAP

b) CPMIA d) CIPMA

63. Directorate of Medicinal and Aromatic Plants Research is located at

a) Anand c) Boriavi

b) Gandhinagar d) Ahmedabad

64. Jawahar Lal Nehru Tropical Botanical Garden and Research Institute is located at

a) Mysore c) Chennai

b) Thiruvananthapuram d) Coimbatore

65. National Medicinal Plant Board is abbreviated as

a) NMPB c) NPMB

b) NPBM d) NBPM

66. National Medicinal Plant Board is operational under the department of

a) Homeopathy c) Biotechnology

b) AYUSH d) Siddha

67. National Medicinal Plant Board is located at

a) Mumbai c) Kanpur

b) Pondicherry d) New Delhi

68. The premier institute (CDRI) that works on Pharmacology and clinical trials of Medicinal plants is located at

a) Mumbai c) Delhi

b) Lucknow d) Chennai

69. Council of Scientific and Industrial Research is located at

a) Karnal c) New Delhi

b) Indore d) Chandigarh

70. NCL is located at National Chemical Laboratory

a) Nasik c) Dapoli

b) Aurangabad d) Pune

71. National Mission on Medicinal Plants is governed by

a) National Medicinal Plant Board

c) National Biodiversity Board

b) National Biodiversity Authority

d) All of these

72. The main mandates of IUCN are

a) Documentation of Biodiversity

b) Conservation of Biodiversity

c) Framing strategies for Biodiversity management

d) All of these

73. The headquarter of WHO is located at
    a) Greece c) Geneva
    b) Rome d) Sweden
74. Ayurvedic Drug Manufacturing Association is abbreviated as
    a) AMAD c) ADAM
    b) ADMA d) AADM
75. The headquarter of FAO is located at
    a) Rome c) Peru
    b) San Francisco d) Chille
76. CBD stands for
    a) Convention of Bird Diversity
    b) Convention on Biodiversity
    c) Convention on Biological Diversity
    d Both B and C
77. CBD came into existence in the year
    a) 1993 c) 1991
    b) 1992 d) 1990
78. Bark of which of the following tree species is most widely used in treating cardiac problems?
    a) *Terminalia arjuna* c) *Terminalia catappa*
    b) *Terminalia chebula* d) *Terminalia bellerica*
79. The alkaloids Strychnine and Brucine are obtained from
    a) *Strychnos potatorum* c) *Strychnos longifolia*
    b) *Strychnos nux vomica* d) Both a and b
80. Which plant part of *Caesalpinia sappan* yields orange red dye stuff?
    a) Seeds c) Leaves
    b) Heart wood d) Pods
81. Which of the following plant species is native to Eastern China and India?
    a) *Curcuma longa* c) *Curcuma zeodaria*
    b) *Curcuma domestica* d) *Curcuma amada*

82. Cardiac glycosides are obtained from
    a) Indian Foxglove plant
    b) *Digitalis purpurea*
    c) Both A and B
    d) Only B

83. How many licensed Ayurvedic drugs manufacturing unit are operational in India?
    a) 7600
    b) 7500
    c) 5600
    d) 7000

84. How many species of *Ocimum* are found in India?
    a) 05
    b) 06
    c) 07
    d) 09

85. Totality of all living organisms is called
    a) Biological Diversity
    b) Biological Potential
    c) Biological Fecundity
    d) Carrying capacity

86. What are the different levels of Biodiversity?
    a) 02
    b) 04
    c) 05
    d) 03

87. The listing of Rare and Endangered Medicinal plants is called
    a) Blue data book
    b) Black data book
    c) Red data book
    d) Green data book

88. Colchicine is obtained from
    a) *Colchicium luteum*
    b) *Gloriosa superba*
    c) Both A and B
    d) Only A

89. Chemically Colchicine is
    a) Terpenoids
    b) Alkaloids
    c) Phenols
    d) Dyes

90. Colchicine is mainly used for
    a) Chromosome studies
    b) Cell studies
    c) To change chromosome numbers
    d) All of these

91. Withanolides is mainly extracted from
    a) *Withania coagulans* c) Both A and B
    b) *Withania somnifera* d) Only B
92. Catharitine and Vinolidine sulphate are extracted from
    a) *Vinca rosea* c) *Lochnera rosea*
    b) *Vinca rosea* var. *alba* d) All of these
93. Vincristine and vinblastine are classified as
    a) Indole alkaloids
    b) Pyridine Piperidine alkaloids
    c) Tropane alkaloids
    d) True alkaloids
94. Withaferine and Withasomnine are classified as
    a) Pseudo alkaloids c) Indole alkaloids
    b) Proto alkaloids d) Tropane alkaloids
95. Botanical name of Black Zedoary is
    a) *Curcuma caesia* c) *Curcuma aromatica*
    b) *Curcuma zeodaria* d) *Curcuma longa*
96. The economically important part of *Gloriosa superba* is
    a) Seeds c) Rhizomes
    b) Tubers d) Both seeds and Tubers
97. For the commercial cultivation, *Gymnema sylvestre* is best propagated by
    a) Seeds c) Grafting
    b) Root cuttings d) Stem cuttings
98. The largest class of natural compounds found in phenols are
    a) Chalcones c) Flavanones
    b) Quinones d) Flavols
99. RRL – 011 is the improved variety of
    a) *Ocimum bascilicum* c) *Ocimum cloviscens*
    b) *Ocimum sanctum* d) *Ocimum canum*

100. Alkaloids obtained from kalmegh / king of bitter are called
   a) Withanolides c) Isoquinoline alkaloids
   b) Andrographaloides d) Bitter alkaloids

101. Alkaloids Hyoscyamine and Atropine can be obtained from
   a) *Atropa belladonna* c) *Datura metal*
   b) *Hyocyamus niger* d) *Aconitum ferox*

102. Which plant part of *Atropa belladonna* has sedative, stimulant and antispasmodic properties?
   a) Leaves c) Bark
   b) Fruit d) Root

103. Which part of belladonna yields toxic alkaloids?
   a) Fruit c) Leaves
   b) Bark d) Root

104. Which plant part of Sarpagandha is medicinally important?
   a) Bark c) Leaves
   b) Root d) Seeds

105. Which plant is medicinally used in reducing blood pressure?
   a) *Rauwolfia serpentina* c) *Rauwolfia canescens*
   b) *Rauwolfia tetraphylla* d) *Rauwolfia vomitoria*

106. According to ancient ayurvedic literature, which plant is considered as potential antidote against snake bite and insect stings?
   a) Ashwagandha c) Kawanch
   b) Bael d) Sarpagandha

107. Which part of Sarpagandha is useful as an antidote for snake poison?
   a) Fruit c) Root
   b) Leaves d) Stem

108. Which plant is commonly / popularly known as "*Pagal-ki-dawa*" in India?
   a) *Withania somnifera* c) *Rauwolfia serpentina*
   b) *Asparagus racemosus* d) *Centella asiatica*

109. Sarpagandha can be best grown in
   a) Cold and dry conditions
   b) Cold and wet conditions
   c) Hot and dry conditions
   d) Hot and humid conditions

110. Seeds of which medicinal plant is used in the treatment of paralysis and nervous disorder?
   a) *Strychnos nux vomica*
   b) *Crocus sativus*
   c) *Mucuna prurita*
   d) *Ricinus communis*

111. *Strychnos nux vomica* belongs to which plant family?
   a) Euphorbiaceae
   b) Asteraceae
   c) Loganiaceae
   d) Zingiberaceae

112. *Tricholepis zeylanicus* subsp. *travan coricus* – a plant used by the Kani tribe of Southern India has which medicinal properties?
   a) Antifatigue
   b) Provides rejuvenation
   c) Immuno modulator
   d) All of these

113. *Tricholepis zeylanicus* subsp. *travan coricus* is endemic to
   a) Eastern Ghats
   b) Western Ghats
   c) Andaman forests
   d) North east India

114. Which of the following are tropical medicinal plants?
   a) *Chlorophytum borivilianum*
   b) *Curculigo orchioides*
   c) *Gloriosa superba*
   d) All of these

115. Which of the premier institute compiled / listed 427 endangered medicinal plants species?
   a) Botanical Survey of India
   b) Forest Research Institute
   c) FRLHT: Full Form
   d) NBPGR : Full Form

116. Pyridine – Piperidine alkaloids are more abundantly found in
   a) *Piper longum*
   b) *Piper nigrum*
   c) *Piper cubeba*
   d) *Piper betel*

117. *Costus speciosus* belongs to family
   a) Malvaceae
   b) Lamiaceae
   c) Scitaminaceae
   d) Euphorbiaceae

118. Which of the following medicinal plant is widely used as to cure Parkinson's disease?

a) *Mucuna pruriens* c) None of these

b) *Mucuna prurita* d) Both A and B

119. How many species of *Aloe* are commercially used for medicinal purposes?

a) 02 c) 04

b) 03 d) 05

120. Which among the following is the most promising sector in herbal drugs research?

a) Cosmecueticals c) Both A and B

b) Nuetraceuticals d) Only B

121. The wet rhizome yield in *Curcuma amada* is

a) 50 – 65 quintals c) 40-50 quintals

b) 70-80 quintals d) 85-90 quintals

122. Other than C, H and N, alkaloids also contains

a) Sulphur c) Phosphorus

b) Oxygen d) Potassium

123. Terpenes with five carbon atoms is called

a) Monoterpenoids c) Hemiterpenoids

b Di Terpenoids d) Tri Terpenoids

124. Terpenes with infinite carbon atoms is called

a) Poly Terpenoids c) Di Terpenoids

b) Tri Terpenoids d) All of these

125. Botanical name of Alexandrian Senna is

a) *Cassia senna* c) *Cassis occidentalis*

b) *Cassia tora* d) *Cassia acutifolia*

126. Botanical name of Indian senna plant is

a) *Cassia javanica* c) *Cassia angustifolia*

b) *Cassia senna* d) *Cassia italica*

127. *Adhatoda vasica* / *Justicia adhatoda* belongs to family
   a) Orchidaceae
   b) Acanthaceae
   c) Verbenaceae
   d) Zingiberaceae
128. The major chemical constituents found in *Aloe* is
   a) Barbalion
   b) Iso barbalion
   c) Both of these
   d) None of these
129. The major alkaloids found in *Justicia adhatoda vasica* are
   a) Vasicine
   b) Vasicinol
   c) Ephedrine
   d) Both A and B
130. CITES stands for
   a) Convention on International Trade in Endangered species of wild flora and wild fauna
   b) Convention on International Trade of Economically important species
   c) Convention on International Trade of European species
   d) Convention on International Trade of Endemic species
131. FRLHT (Foundation for Revitalization of Local Health Tradition) is located at
   a) Mysore
   b) Ajmer
   c) Cuttack
   d) Bangalore / Bengaluru
132. Central Council for Research in Ayurveda and Siddha (CCRAS) is located at
   a) Hyderabad
   b) New Delhi
   c) Mumbai
   d) Chennai
133. Central Council for Research in Homeopathy (CCRH) is located at
   a) New Delhi
   b) Chandigarh
   c) Patna
   d) Coimbatore
134. ICMR stands for
   a) Indian Centre for Mango Research
   b) Indian Centre for Mustard Research
   c) International Council on Mulberry Research
   d) Indian Council of Medical Research

135. Glory lily is the English common name of
a) *Crinum latifolium*
b) *Pancratium* sp.
c) *Gloriosa superba*
d) *Ensete superbum*

136. HPTLC stands for
a) High Pressure Liquid Chromatography
b) High Performance Thin Layer Chromatography
c) High Pressure Thin Layer Chromatography
d) Both B and C

137. The method of chromatography was invented by
a) T. Swett
b) Swedberg
c) Watson and Crick
d) Madam Curie

138. Which of the following is better in separation as far as Chromatography is concerned?
a) Paper Chromatography
b) Thin Layer Chromatography
c) High Performance Liquid Chromatorgraphy
d) Gas Chromatography combined with Mass Spectroscopy

139. Which among the following is used routinely as adsorbent in Thin Layer Chromatography?
a) Calcium hydroxide
b) Potassium Hydroxide
c) Silica gel with Gypsum
d) Silica gel

140. Which principles are involved in the technique of Chromatography?
a) Adsorption
b) Capillary action
c) Partition Coefficient and Dissociation Constant
d) All of these

141. Which is the main ingredient of the famous ayurvedic preparation Dashmoolarisht?
a) *Aegle marmelos*
b) *Butea monosperma*
c) *Desmodium gangeticum*
d) Both A and C

142. Botanical name of Margosa tree is the English common name of which of the most important medicinal plant?

a) *Melia azaderach* c) *Azadirachta indica*

b) *Melia composita* d) *Melia dubia*

143. As per the WHO guidelines of Quality Assurance and Quality Control of Medicinal plants, all the test should be conducted at temperature range of

a) 15^0C c) 35^0C

b) 25^0C d) 45^0C

144. PCR stands for

a) Polymerase Carbonated Reaction

b) Polymerase Calcium Reaction

c) Polymerized Carbon Reaction

d) Polymerase Chain Reaction

145. How many types of Gas Chromatography are available for identification and separation of compounds?

a) 01 c) 03

b) 04 d) 02

146. Which is the most common spray reagent used for the detection of Alkaloids in Thin Layer Chromatography?

a) Dragendroff's reagent c) Mollisch's reagent

b) Wagner's reagent d) Both A and B

147. The study of crude drugs from medicinal plants is called as

a) Pharmaceutical sciences c) Pharmacology

b) Pharmacy d) Pharmacognosy

148. Which among the following techniques gives the identification of functional chemical groups and bonding patterns?

a) UV Visible Spectroscopy

b) Atomic Absorption Spectroscopy

c) Infra Red Spectroscopy

d) Nuclear Magnetic Resonance

149. The technique of spectroscopy or spectrophotometry is governed by the principle of

a) Beer Lambert's law c) Newton's law
b) Bohr's law d) Bouger Lambert's law

150. PCR technique is used for

a) DNA sample quantification c) DNA amplification
b) Visualize DNA samples d) For hybridization

151. The major limitation of RAPD is which of the following?

a) Reproducibility c) Cost
b) Tediousness d) Sequence information

152. Male sterility, one of the major breakthroughs in plant breeding was observed in which medicinal plant?

a) *Datura alba* c) *Datura stramonium*
b) *Datura metal* d) All of these

153. Northern blotting techniques is used for blotting

a) DNA samples c) Protein samples
b) RNA samples d) All of above

154. Southern blotting techniques is used for blotting

a) Protein samples c) RNA samples
b) DNA samples d) All of above

155. The term germplasm was coined by

a) Weistmann c) Vavilov
b) Harland d) Roberts

156. Which agency is responsible / associated with quarantine of medicinal plant germplasm imported for medicinal purposes or research purposes?

a) National Bureau of Plant Genetic Resources
b) Council of Scientifical Industrial Research
c) Forests Research Instititute
d) Directorate of Plant Protection, Quarantine & Storage

157. Which of the following is non – PCR based molecular marker?

a) RAPD
b) AFLP
c) RFLP
d) STMS

158. Bark of which medicinal plant is used for curing diarrhoea in childrens?

a) *Terminalia arjuna*
b) *Psidium guajava*
c) *Azadirachta indica*
d) *Syzygium cumini*

159. The major chemical compounds found in *Asparagus racemosus* are

a) Sapogenins
b) Saponins
c) Both saponins and sapogenins
d) Various forms of Shataverins

160. Head quarter of Directorate of Plant protection, Quarantine and Storage is located at

a) Aurangabad
b) Bangalore
c) Faridabad
d) Dehradun

161. Protection of genetic diversity of medicinal plants from genetic erosion is defined as

a) Conservation
b) Extinction
c) Collection
d) Exploration

162. RAPD is elaborated as

a) Randomly annealed polymorphic DNA
b) Randomly associated polymorphic DNA
c) Randomly amplified polymorphic DNA
d) Randomly added polymorphic DNA

163. Which type of marker is RAPD?

a) Recessive type of marker
b) Dominant marker
c) Co-dominant marker
d) Both B and C

164. PCR (Polymerase Chain Reaction), one of the most important tool used in molecular biology was invented by

a) Kary Mullis
b) Krens
c) Fodor
d) Roberts

165. Cryopreservation is beneficial when
 a) Seeds are heterozygous
 b) Seeds remain viable only for limited time
 c) Plants do not produce viable seeds
 d) All of these

166. The headquarter of National Biodiversity Authority (NBA) is located at
 a) New Delhi c) Chennai
 b) Pune d) Allahabad

167. The headquarter of Botanical Survey of India (BSI), a premier institute engaged in the collection, identification and maintenance of important forest medicinal plants is located at
 a) Itarsi c) Jammu
 b) Varanasi d) Kolkatta

168. Conservation of medicinal plants in its natural habitat where it is distributed is called
 a) *Ex situ* conservation c) *In vitro* conservation
 b) *In situ* conservation d) *In vivo* conservation

169. Conservation of medicinal plants outside its natural area of occurrence or distribution is called
 a) *In vitro* conservation c) *Ex situ* conservation
 b) *In vivo* conservation d) *In situ* conservation

170. Which variety of *Cassia senna* developed by CIMAP (Lucknow) is recommended for North Indian Plains?
 a) Sona c) ALFT-1
 b) AFTL-1 d) ALFT-2

171. ALFT-2 variety of *Cassia senna* recommended for growing exclusively as leaf crop is developed by
 a) Navsari Agricultural University, Navasari
 b) Gujarat Agricultural University, Anand
 c) Junagadh Agricultural University, Junagadh
 d) MPUAT, Udaipur

172. Which of the following conditions hinder the crop production in *Catharanthus roseus*?
   a) Low winter temperature
   b) Saline soils
   c) Water logged or highly alkaline soils
   d) All of these

173. The chromosome complement in Indian Periwinkle is
   a) 2n = 8
   b) 2n = 10
   c) 2n = 16
   d) 2n = 12

174. Forskolin, isolated from roots of *Coleus forskohlii* is useful in
   a) Broncho dilator
   b) Congestive heart failure
   c) Thrombosis and Glaucoma therapy
   d) All of these

175. Which type of soil condition favours the growth and yield of Ashwagandha?
   a) Loamy
   b) Black alluvial
   c) Sandy loam and light red soils
   d) Waterlogged soils

176. Under AICRP on medicinal and aromatic plants, how many plant selections were made for *Withania somnifera*?
   a) 100
   b) 150
   c) 175
   d) 200

177. *Gloriosa superba* is
   a) Moderately rooted plant
   b) Deep rooted plant
   c) Shallow rooted plant
   d) None of these

178. Chromosome complement in *Aloe barbadenss* is
   a) 2n = 8
   b) 2n = 14
   c) 2n = 12
   d) 2n = 16

179. *Aloe* species are tolerant to
   a) Higher pH with low Na and K salts
   b) Lower pH with low Na and K salts
   c) Lower pH with high Na and K salts
   d) Higher pH with high Na and K salts

180. Curacao aloe is obtained from
   a) *Aloe vera*
   b) *Aloe perryi*
   c) *Aloe barbadensis*
   d) *Aloe ferox*

181. Roots of which of the following medicinal plant is banned to be exported from India under CITES?
   a) *Datura alba*
   b) *Rauwolfia serpentina*
   c) *Withania somnifera*
   d) *Asparagus racemosus* var. *javanicus*

182. Which alkaloid extracted from Sarpagandha is widely used in herbal industry?
   a) Ajmaline
   b) Serpentinine
   c) Serpentine
   d) All of these

183. Basic chromosome number of *Dioscorea composita* and *Dioscorea floribunda* is
   a) n = 4
   b) n = 9
   c) n = 8
   d) n = 6

184. Which type of soil restricts the tuber growth in *Dioscorea* spp?
   a) Loamy soils
   b) Alluvial soils
   c) Heavy clay and acidic soils
   d) Red soils

185. With increase in light intensity, which of the following attributes is affected in *Andrographis paniculata*?
   a) Andrographolid content
   b) Chlorophyll content
   c) Seed size
   d) Biomass

186. Maximum biomass yield can be obtained in *Andrographis paniculata* by applying
   a) Neem cake
   b) Vermicompost
   c) N as urea
   d) N as castor cake

187. Somatic chromosome number reported in *Piper longum* is

a) 2n = 24
c) 2n = 52
b) 2n = 48
d) All of these

188. Based on the size and taste, how many varieties of *Piper* are recognized in trade?

a) 02
c) 03
b) 04
d) 05

189. Commercial cultivation of Isabgol (*Plantago ovata*) is mainly confined to which districts in Gujarat?

a) Vadodara & Panchmahals
c) Sabarkantha and Mehsana
b) Surat and Narmada
d) Mehsana and Banaskantha

190. Basic chromosome number in *Plantago ovata* is

a) n = 4
c) n = 8
b) n = 5
d) n = 9

191. Opium poppy is native of

a) Asia minor
b) Madagascar
c) Western Mediterranean Europe
d) Afghanistan and Iran

192. Somatic chromosome number reported in *Chlorophytum borivilianum* is

a) 2n = 12
c) 2n = 24
b) 2n = 16
d) 2n = 48

193. During storage, tubers of *Chlorophytum borivilianum* is mainly infected by

a) *Aspergillus* spp
c) Both A and B
b) *Fusarium* spp
d) None of these

194. Steviosides are how many times sweeter than normal table sugar?

a) 200
c) 300
b) 100
d) 400

195. Botanical name of Cochin oil grass is
   a) *Cymbopogon pendula*
   b) *Cymbopogon flexuosus*
   c) *Cymbopogon citratus*
   d) *Cymbopogon khasianum*

196. Botanical name of Japanese mint is
   a) *Mentha spicata*
   b) *Mentha citrata*
   c) *Mentha arvensis*
   d) *Mentha piperita*

197. *Pelargonium graveolens* (Geranium) is native of
   a) India
   b) South East America
   c) Mediterranean regions
   d) Cape region of South Africa

198. Palmarosa grows well with soil pH of
   a) 6.0 – 6.5
   b) 5.5 – 6.0
   c) 6.5 – 7.0
   d) 5.0 – 5.5

199. Which one of the following is the highly sophisticated recent technology for extraction of volatile oils?
   a) Supercritical fluid extraction
   b) High performance thin layer chromatography
   c) Gas Chromatography
   d) Solvent extraction

200. Which of the following plant is endemic as well as medicinally highly valuable?
   a) *Pinus roxburghii*
   b) *Ephedra foliata*
   c) *Taxus baccata*
   d) *Ginkgo biloba*

Answer Key

1.	**b**	2.	**a**	3.	**d**	4.	**a**	5.	**c**	6.	**b**	7.	**d**	8.	**c**
9.	**a**	10.	**b**	11.	**a**	12.	**d**	13.	**b**	14.	**c**	15.	**a**	16.	**b**
17.	**a**	18.	**c**	19.	**b**	20.	**a**	21.	**c**	22.	**b**	23.	**d**	24.	**c**
25.	**a**	26.	**b**	27.	**c**	28.	**d**	29.	**b**	30.	**d**	31.	**b**	32.	**d**
33.	**b**	34.	**a**	35.	**a**	36.	**d**	37.	**c**	38.	**b**	39.	**d**	40.	**c**
41.	**d**	42.	**b**	43.	**d**	44.	**b**	45.	**d**	46.	**c**	47.	**a**	48.	**d**
49.	**b**	50.	**d**	51.	**b**	52.	**a**	53.	**d**	54.	**c**	55.	**a**	56.	**c**
57.	**b**	58.	**d**	59.	**a**	60.	**b**	61.	**d**	62.	**a**	63.	**c**	64.	**b**
65.	**a**	66.	**b**	67.	**d**	68.	**b**	69.	**c**	70.	**d**	71.	**a**	72.	**d**
73.	**c**	74.	**b**	75.	**a**	76.	**d**	77.	**b**	78.	**a**	79.	**c**	80.	**b**
81.	**d**	82.	**c**	83.	**b**	84.	**b**	85.	**a**	86.	**d**	87.	**c**	88.	**c**
89.	**b**	90.	**d**	91.	**b**	92.	**d**	93.	**a**	94.	**d**	95.	**a**	96.	**c**
97.	**d**	98.	**b**	99.	**a**	100.	**b**	101.	**a**	102.	d	103.	**c**	104.	**b**
105.	**a**	106.	**d**	107.	**b**	108.	**c**	109.	**d**	110.	**a**	111.	**c**	112.	**d**
113.	**b**	114.	**d**	115.	**a**	116.	**d**	117.	**c**	118.	**d**	119.	**b**	120.	**a**
121.	**c**	122.	**b**	123.	**c**	124.	**a**	125.	**d**	126.	**c**	127.	**b**	128.	**c**
129.	**d**	130.	**a**	131.	**d**	132.	**b**	133.	**a**	134.	**d**	135.	**c**	136.	**b**
137.	**a**	138.	**d**	139.	**c**	140.	**a**	141.	**d**	142.	**c**	143.	**a**	144.	**d**
145.	**b**	146.	**a**	147.	**d**	148.	**c**	149.	**a**	150.	**c**	151.	**a**	152.	**d**
153.	**c**	154.	**b**	155.	**a**	156.	**d**	157.	**c**	158.	**b**	159.	**d**	160.	**c**
161.	**a**	162.	**c**	163.	**b**	164.	**a**	165.	**d**	166.	**c**	167.	**d**	168.	**b**
169.	**c**	170.	**a**	171.	**b**	172.	**d**	173.	**c**	174.	**d**	175.	**c**	176.	**d**
177.	**c**	178.	**b**	179.	**d**	180.	**c**	181.	**b**	182.	**a**	183.	**b**	184.	**c**
185.	**b**	186.	**c**	187.	**d**	188.	**b**	189.	**d**	190.	**b**	191.	**c**	192.	**b**
193.	**c**	194.	**a**	195.	**b**	196.	**c**	197.	**d**	198.	**c**	199.	**a**	200.	**d**

4

Introductory Botany

1. A word related to any non woody plant is called
   a) Herbaceous
   b) Woody
   c) Soft
   d) Green
2. Stem that remains above ground in air is called
   a) Strong
   b) Woody
   c) Aerial
   d) Erect
3. A strong and hard stem in upright position is called
   a) Diffuse
   b) Erect
   c) Woody
   d) Non woody
4. A positively geotropic leafless lower portion of the plant axis is called
   a) Stem
   b) Root
   c) Flower
   d) Leaf
5. Root arising directly from the is called radicle
   a) Normal
   b) Adventitious
   c) Both of these
   d) None of these
6. Aerial roots are found in
   a) Orchids
   b) Mango
   c) Sweet potato
   d) All of these
7. Acicular leaf is found in
   a) *Cycas*
   b) *Pinus*
   c) Rose
   d) Neem

8. Midrib is also called as
   a) Leaf c) Costa
   b) Leaflets d) Petiole
9. The study of external features of plants is called as
   a) Taxonomy c) Both of these
   b) Morphology d) None of these
10. Carl Linnaeus is rightly called as Father of
   a) Father of taxonomy c) Father of biology
   b) Father of genetics d) Father of zoology
11. Stem is
   a) Negatively geotropic c) Both of these
   b) Positively phototropic d) None of these
12. Root is
   a) Positively geotropic c) Both of these
   b) Negatively phototropic d) None of these
13. *Avicennia* is an example of
   a) Orchids c) Parasites
   b) Mangroves d) Epiphytes
14. Plants that grows on rocks are called as
   a) Psammophytes c) Hydrophytes
   b) Lithophytes d) Mesophytes
15. Tuber is a modification of
   a) Root c) Leaf
   b) Stem d) Flower
16. Opposite phyllotaxy is found in
   a) *Hibiscus rosa sinensis* c) *Azadirachta indica*
   b) *Vinca rosea* d) Cynodon *dactylon*
17. 2/5 alternate phyllotaxy is found in
   a) *Datura alba* c) *Hibiscus rosa sinensis*
   b) *Mimosa pudica* d) *Polyalthia longifolia*

18. Tendrils are modification of
    - a) Stem
    - b) Leaf
    - c) Root
    - d) Both A & B
19. Orchids are examples of
    - a) Monocots
    - b) Parasites
    - c) Epiphytes
    - d) Both A & C
20. Inflorescence is
    - a) Arrangement of flowers
    - b) Arrangement of seeds
    - c) Arrangement of ovary
    - d) Arrangement of leaves
21. Tepals are part of
    - a) Calyx
    - b) Corolla
    - c) Perianth
    - d) Bracts
22. Petals are part of
    - a) Perianth
    - b) Calyx
    - c) Corolla
    - d) Bracteoles
23. Sepals are part of
    - a) Corolla
    - b) Perianth
    - c) Bracts & bracteoles
    - d) Calyx
24. Plants that complete their life cycle in one single year are called
    - a) Perennials
    - b) Biennial
    - c) Annuals
    - d) Ephemerals
25. Botanical name of is Sadabahar/Indian Pericoinkle
    - a) *Catharanthus roseus*
    - b) *Vinca rosea*
    - c) *Lochnera rosea*
    - d) All of these
26. When flower is hypogynous, the position of ovary is
    - a) Inferior
    - b) Superior
    - c) Half inferior half superior
    - d) All of these
27. When flower is epigynous, the position of ovary is
    - a) Superior
    - b) Half superior
    - c) Inferior
    - d) Half inferior

28. When flower has all floral parts in multiples of 3, it is called
    a) Pentamerous
    b) Tetramerous
    c) Trimerous
    d) Dimerous
29. When flower has all floral parts in multiples of 5, it is called
    a) Trimerous
    b) Dimerous
    c) Pentamerous
    d) Tetramerous
30. Plants that grow in acidic soil are called
    a) Oxylophytes
    b) Basophytes
    c) Lithophytes
    d) Parasites
31. Plants that grow in desert conditions is called
    a) Lithophytes
    b) Xerophytes
    c) Mesophytes
    d) Hydrophytes
32. Leaf without petiole is called
    a) Sessile
    b) Apetiolate
    c) Sub sessile
    d) Both A & B
33. The arrangement of veins & vein lets is called
    a) Aestivation
    b) Venation
    c) Placentation
    d) Phyllotaxy
34. Seed is defined as
    a) Matured flower
    b) Matured ovule
    c) Matured fruit
    d) Matured embryo
35. Fruit is defined as
    a) Matured embryo
    b) Matured ovary
    c) Matured flower
    d) Matured ovule
36. Plants that grow in water are called as
    a) Halophytes
    b) Mesophytes
    c) Hydrophytes
    d) Psammophytes
37. *Vanda* is an example of
    a) Epiphytic orchid
    b) Grasses
    c) Terrestrial orchid
    d) Both a and c

38. If the flowers are arranged on lateral branches the inflorescence is called

a) Cyathiom c) Raceme

b) Verticillaster d) Cymose

39. Arrangement of calyx and corolla in a flower of Floral bud is called

a) Aestivation c) Venation

b) Placentation d) All of these

40. Arrangement of ovules in ovary is called

a) Phyllotaxy c) Inflorescence

b) Placentation d) None of these

41. Arrangement of leaves on the main axis is called

a) Venation c) Phyllotaxy

b) Placentation d) Phyllotaxis

42. The sterile stamens are called

a) Anthers c) Infertile stamens

b) Staminodes d) None of these

43. The organ that produces sperms in Mosses and Ferns is called

a) Gamentangia c) Antheridia

b) Zygote d) Archegonia

44. Sundew and pitcher plant are examples of

a) Parasitic plants c) Photosynthetic plants

b) Insectivorous plants d) Both a and c

45. The sporophyte in the seed plant is

a) Haploid c) Hexaploid

b) Diploid d) Tetraploid

46. The study of algae is called

a) Mycology c) Bryology

b) Algology d) Botany

47. The study of fungi is called

a) Bryology c) Mycology

b) Botany d) Algology

48. Branch of botany dealing with the study of plant tissues is called

a) cell biology
c) Parasitology
b) Histology
d) Anatomy

49. Genetics is the branch that deals with the study of

a) Chromosomes
c) Variation
b) Heredity
d) Both B & C

50. The binomial system of nomenclature was introduced by

a) G. M. Smith
c) Hooker
b) Brandis
d) Carl Linnaeus

51. Branch of botany that deals with study of cell is called

a) Genetics
c) Cytology
b) Cell biology
d) Both B & C

52. Double fertilization is the common feature of

a) Angiosperms
c) Pteridophytes
b) Gymnosperms
d) Bryophytes

53. Sugarcane is the example of

a) Dicot plant
c) Both of these
b) Monocot plant
d) None of these

54. Sunflower is the example of

a) Monocot plant
c) Angiosperm plant
b) Dicot plant
d) Both B & C

55. Plants that bears flowers and seeds are called

a) Cryptogams
c) Phanerogams
b) Angiosperms
d) Gymnosperms

56. Plants that do not bear seeds and flowers are called

a) Phanerogams
c) Cryptogams
b) Thallophytes
d) Both B & C

57. Plants with naked seed are called

a) Dicotyledons
c) Angiosperms
b) Monocotyledons
d) Gymnosperms

58. Plants which prefer light to grow are called
    a) Sciophytes c) Parasites
    b) Heliophytes d) Epiphytes
59. Plants that do not prefer light to grow are called as
    a) Epiphytes c) Heliophytes
    b) Sciophytes d) Parasites
60. *Cycas* is an example of
    a) Angiosperms c) Thallophytes
    b) Monocotyledons d) Gymnosperms
61. *Cuscuta* is an example of
    a) Total stem parasite c) Partial root parasite
    b) Total root parasite d) Partial stem parasite
62. Algae and fungi are examples of
    a) Non flowering plants c) Thallophytes
    b) Flowering plants d) Both A & C
63. Plants that grow on dead and decaying material are called as
    a) Halophytes c) Saprophytes
    b) Psammophytes d) Lichens
64. Vascular bundles with cambium are called
    a) Closed c) Collateral
    b) Open d) Bicollateral
65. Vascular bundles without cambium are called
    a) Closed c) Open
    b) Radial d) Collateral
66. 3/8 alternate phyllotaxy is found in
    a) Mango c) Chinorose
    b) Papaya d) Rose
67. Flower is a modified for sexual reproduction
    a) Leaf c) Stem
    b) Bracts d) Shoot

68. If the flower has all essential floral parts it is called
    a) Incomplete c) Regular
    b) Complete d) Irregular

69. Male flower is also called
    a) Pistillate c) Unisexual
    b) Bisexual d) Staminate

70. Female flower is also called
    a) Bisexual c) Staminate
    b) Pistillate d) Unisexual

71. Autogamy means
    a) Cross pollination c) Self pollination
    b) Self fertilization d) Cross fertilization

72. Allogamy means
    a) Self pollination c) Cross pollination
    b) Self fertilization d) Cross fertilization

73. Pollination by wind is called
    a) Zoophily c) Entemophily
    b) Anemophily d) Myrophylii

74. Pollination by water is called
    a) Hydrophily c) Myrophylii
    b) Zoophily d) Entemophily

75. Pollination by insects is called
    a) Entemophily c) Anemophily
    b) Hydrophily d) None of these

76. Pollination by animals is called
    a) Anemophily c) Hydrophily
    b) Zoophily d) All of these

77. The morphological nature of the edible part of coconut is
    a) Thalamus c) Endocarp
    b) Mesocarp d) Endosperm

78. The embryo sac develops within the
    a) Embryo c) Pollen grain
    b) Endosperm d) Ovule
79. Phylloclade is an aerial modification of
    a) Petiole c) Stipule
    b) Stem d) Leaf base
80. Hypanthodium is
    a) An ordinary hypocotyl
    b) A placentation
    c) A special type of inflorescence
    d) A special type of fruit
81. Phyllode is
    a) Modified root c) Modified leaf
    b) Modified shoot d) Modified petiole
82. Transfer of pollen from anthers to stigma is called
    a) Aestivation c) Fertilization
    b) Pollination d) Reproduction
83. Which is the most essential requirement for the germination of seed?
    a) Light c) Water
    b) Low temperature d) Oxygen
84. Ovary with two chambers is called
    a) Unilocular c) Trilocular
    b) Bilocular d) Multilocular
85. Cyathium is a type of
    a) Arrangement of flowers c) Arrangement of tissue
    b) Arrangement of ovules d) None of these
86. Parallel venation is commonly found in
    a) Monocotyledons c) Dicotyledons
    b) Angiosperms d) Gymnosperms

87. A compound raceme is called
   a) Umbel
   B Panicle
   c) Corymbs
   d) Spadix

88. The peduncle is the
   a) Fruit stalk
   b) Part of seed
   c) Part of ovary
   d) Flower axis

89. Flowers that cannot be divided into two equal halves are called
   a) Cyclic
   b) Monocyclic
   c) Regular
   d) Zygomorphic

90. Flowers that can be divided into two equal halves are called
   a) Regular
   b) Irregular
   c) Actinomorphic
   d) Both A & C

91. A parthenocarpic fruit has
   a) No seeds
   b) Seed without seed coat
   c) Seed with seed coat
   d) All of these

92. Caryopsis is
   a) Type of fruit
   b) Type of flower
   c) Type of seed
   d) Type of pollination

93. The embryo consists of
   a) Only cotyledons
   b) Only plumule
   c) Cotyledons, radical, plumule
   d) None of these

94. The group of cells present in the apical part of root and stem are called
   a) Apical meristems
   b) Lateral meristems
   c) Intercalary meristems
   d) Primary meristems

95. Most important component of phloem is
   a) Seive tube
   b) Sieve cells
   c) Companion cells
   d) Phloem fibres

96. Sclrenchyma is
   a) Mechanical tissue
   b) Complex tissue
   c) Simple tissue
   d) Permanent tissue
97. Rhizome is found in
   a) Garlic
   b) Onion
   c) Ginger
   d) Both B & C
98. Velamen tissue are found commonly in
   a) Parasites
   b) Epiphytes
   c) Mesophytes
   d) All of these
99. Plants that grow in saline conditions are called
   a) Hydrophytes
   b) Epiphytes
   c) Halophytes
   d) Psammophytes
100. The only monocot in which the cambium is present is
   a) *Draceana* spp.
   b) *Sachharum* spp.
   c) *Cyperus* spp.
   d) *Yucca* spp.

Answer Key

1.	**a**	2.	**c**	3.	**b**	4.	**b**	5.	**b**	6.	**a**	7.	**b**	8.	**c**
9.	**c**	10.	**a**	11.	**c**	12.	**c**	13.	**b**	14.	**b**	15.	**b**	16.	**b**
17.	**c**	18.	**d**	19.	**d**	20.	**a**	21.	**c**	22.	**c**	23.	**d**	24.	**c**
25.	**d**	26.	**b**	27.	**c**	28.	**c**	29.	**c**	30.	**a**	31.	**b**	32.	**d**
33.	**b**	34.	**b**	35.	**b**	36.	**c**	37.	a	38.	**c**	39.	**a**	40.	**b**
41.	**c**	42.	**b**	43.	**c**	44.	**b**	45.	**b**	46.	**b**	47.	**c**	48.	**b**
49.	**d**	50.	**d**	51.	**b**	52.	**a**	53.	**b**	54.	**b**	55.	**c**	56.	**c**
57.	**d**	58.	**b**	59.	**b**	60.	**d**	61.	**a**	62.	**d**	63.	**c**	64.	**b**
65.	**a**	66.	**b**	67.	**d**	68.	**b**	69.	**d**	70.	**b**	71.	**c**	72.	**c**
73.	**b**	74.	**a**	75.	**a**	76.	**b**	77.	**d**	78.	**d**	79.	**b**	80.	**c**
81.	**c**	82.	**b**	83.	**d**	84.	**b**	85.	**a**	86.	**a**	87.	**b**	88.	**d**
89.	**d**	90.	**d**	91.	**a**	92.	**a**	93.	**c**	94.	**a**	95.	**c**	96.	**a**
97.	**c**	98.	**b**	99.	**c**	100.	**a**								

5

Crop Physiology

PAPER-I

1. Osmosis involves
   a) Cell to cell movement of water
   b) Movement of water through cortical cells
   c) Active absorption of water through roots
   d) All of the above
2. In osmosis solvent flows from
   a) Its lower amount to its higher amount
   b) Its higher amount to its lower amount
   c) One cell to another
   d) A dead cell to a living cell
3. The value of DPD of a cell is
   a) OP x TP b) OP + TP
   c) OP – TP d) OP/ TP
4. Osmotic potential of a solution is always
   a) Positive b) Negative
   c) Zero d) Variable
5. Highest value of Ψ_w is (PSI)
   a) 1 b) 0
   c) 10 d) 100
6. Turgidity in a cell is maintained by
   a) Wall pressure b) Diffusion pressure
   c) Turgor pressure d) Osmotic pressure

7. Maximum root pressure is found when
   a) Transpiration is low and absorption is also low
   b) Transpiration is low and absorption is very high
   c) Transpiration is high and absorption is low
   d) Transpiration is high and absorption is very high

8. During the absorption of water by root hairs, the water potential of cell sap is lower than that of
   a) Soil solution but higher than pure water
   b) Pure water and soil solution
   c) Neither pure water nor soil solution
   d) Pure water but higher than soil solution

9. The ultimate cause of water movement against the gravity is
   a) Osmosis b) Imbibition
   c) ATP hydrolysis d) Transpiration

10. The effective adaptation for better gaseous exchange in plant is
   a) Large number of hairs on lower epidermis
   b) Presence of stomata on lower surface of leaf
   c) Multiple epidermis
   d) Waxy cuticle

11. Guttation is caused due to
   a) Imbibition b) Osmosis
   c) Transpiration d) Root Pressure

12. The primary osmolite which causes an opening and closing of stomata is
   a) Sugar b) Starch
   c) K- malate d) Water

13. The guard cells differ from other epidermal cells in having
   a) Mitochondria b) Chloroplast
   c) Nucleus d) Endoplasmic reticulum

14. Which one of the following processes may loss salts from plants?

    a) Guttation b) Transpiration

    c) Both a and b d) None of these

15. Temporary wilting in plants occurs when the rate of water absorption is

    a) Equal to transpiration b) Less than transpiration

    c) More than transpiration d) More than transpiration

16. Guttation takes place through

    a) Wounds b) Lenticles

    c) Hydathodes d) Stomata

17. Two important functions of leaves are

    a) Photosynthesis and respiration

    b) Photoperiodism and transpiration

    c) Transpiration and phototropism

    d) Photosynthesis and guttation

18. Conversion of starch into sugar is essential for

    a) Stomatal closure b) Stomatal opening

    c) Stomatal initiation d) Stomatal ontogeny

19. On the basis of symptoms of chlorosis in leaves a student inferred that this was due to deficiency of nitrogen. This inference could be correct only if yellowing appeared first in

    a) Young leaves

    b) Old leaves

    c) Young leaves followed by old leaves

    d) Old leaves followed by young leaves

20. Absence of Mg^{++} ions from plant tissue results in

    a) Plasmolysis b) Hydrolysis

    c) Chlorosis d) Necrosis

21. Rapid deterioration of root and shoot tips occurs due to deficiency of
    a) Calcium b) Phosphorus
    c) Nitrogen d) Carbon
22. Which of the following statement is correct in reference to micro-essential elements
    a) These are found in small quantities in the soil
    b) These are less important than macro-element
    c) These are toxic at higher concentration and have more importance than macro elements
    d) They are required in very small quantity
23. Flowering plants obtain nitrogen from the soil in the form of
    a) NO_2 b) NO_3
    c) N_2O d) N_2
24. Which of the following is obtained by insectivorous plants from insect bodies?
    a) O_2 b) CO_2
    c) N_2 d) SO_2
25. In C_4 plants, Calvin cycle occurs in
    a) Stroma of bundle sheath chloroplast
    b) Mesophyll chloroplast
    c) Grana of bundle sheath chloroplast
    d) Adverse condition
26. Deficiency symptoms of Mg, Zn, K and N occur first in old leaves which indicates that
    a) These element are non-mobile
    b) These are readily mobile
    c) These are less mobile
    d) These require ATP for their mobility
27. Deficiency of Iron first appears in
    a) Young leaves b) Old leaves
    c) Young fruits d) General starvation

28. The most abundant protein found in the biosphere is met within
   a) Cytosol b) Chloroplast
   c) Aleurone layers d) Legumes

29. The enzyme responsible for CO_2 assimilation in sugarcane is
   a) PEPCO b) Carbonic dehydrogenase
   c) Decarboxylase d) Rubisco

30. The first photochemical reaction in the process of photosynthesis is
   a) Photolysis of water b) Excitation of chlorophyll
   c) Photophosphorylation d) Release of O_2 from water

31. Photolysis of water occurs in association of
   a) PS I b) PS II
   c) Both PS I and PS II d) Matrix

32. Which colour of light is absorbed maximum in photosynthesis?
   a) Red b) Blue
   c) Violet d) Green

33. Tropical grasses like sugarcane show high efficiency of CO_2 fixation because of
   a) Double Calvin cycle b) Photorespiration
   c) Hatch and Slack cycle d) Warburg effect

34. The light and dark reaction of photosynthesis are linked by
   a) RuBP b) Light
   c) $NADPH_2$ d) $NADPH_2$ and ATP

35. Rate of photosynthesis process is independent from
   a) Temperature b) Quality of light
   c) Quantity of light d) Duration of light

36. Which of the following are C_3 plants?
   a) Maize and rice b) Maize and Pineaaple
   c) Oat and barley d) All of these

37. In C_4 cycle, the first step is
  a) CO_2 combine with RuDP b) CO_2 combines with PGA
  c) CO_2 combines with PEP d) CO_2 combines with RMP
38. C_4 plants usually lack
  a) Photorespiration b) Calvin cycle
  c) Both a and b d) Kreb cycle
39. What is common between photosynthesis and respiration?
  a) Cytochromes b) Light
  c) ADP formation d) O_2
40. In respiration there is conversion of
  a) Kinetic into potential energy
  b) Radiant into kinetic energy
  c) Potential into chemical energy
  d) Potential into kinetic energy
41. Krebs cycle takes place in mitochondria, in its
  a) All parts b) Outer membrane
  c) Cristae d) Matrix
42. Photorespiration is favoured by
  a) Low O_2 and high CO_2
  b) High O_2 and low CO_2
  c) Low temperature and high CO_2
  d) Low light and high O_2
43. A cell organelle associated with photorespiration is
  a) Lysosome b) Peroxisome
  c) Glyoxysome d) Ribosome
44. When oilseeds respire, the R.Q. will be
  a) Unity b) More than unity
  c) Less than unity d) All of these
45. The connecting link between glycolysis and Kreb cycle is
  a) Pyruvic acid b) Cytochromes
  c) Acetyl CoA d) Citric acid

46. During aerobic respiration, the substrate which enters the mitochondria is

a) Glucose b) Pyruvic acid

c) Acetyl CoA d) Phosphoglyceraldehyde

47. R.Q. is higher when respiratory substrate is

a) Glucose b) Protein

c) Malic acid d) Fat

48. In photosynthesis and respiration, the energy is derived from

a) Cytochrome and enzymes

b) Phytochromes

c) Electron flow across cytochromes

d) Oxygen

49. The correct sequence of Krebs cycle is

a) Isocitric acid → Oxalosuccinic acid → Citric acid

b) Isocitric acid → Oxalosuccinic acid → α-ketoglutaric acid

c) α- Ketoglutaric acid àIsocitric acid → Oxalosuccinic acid

d) Isocitric acid → α-ketoglutaric acid → Oxalosuccinic acid

50-53 Assume that a plant cell with a water potential of -1.0 MPa is placed in a beaker containing a sucrose solution that has a water potential of -4.0 MPa. Answer the following question.

50. The plant cell will become

a) Large

b) Smaller

c) Not change

d) We can't predict anything from this information

51. The weight of the plant cell will

a) Increase

b) Decrease

c) Not change

d) We can't predict anything from this information

52. The concentration of the sucrose solution in the beaker will
    a) Increase
    b) Decrease
    c) Not change
    d) We can't predict anything from this information
53. After a few hours the cell is removed. A drop of sucrose (-4.0 MPa) placed in the solution, drop will
    a) Float
    b) Sink
    c) Disperse
    d) We can't predict anything from this information
54. ADP from ATP and NADP from NADPH are regenerated from
    a) Hill reaction   b) Photolysis of water
    c) Phtorespiration   d) Calvin cycle
55. Select the correct sequence of events from stomata closed to opening
    a) Stoma closed → decrease water potential → guard cell turgid → water uptake by osmosis → solute potential decreases → pressure increases → K+ uptakeàstoma opens
    b) Stoma closed → water uptake by osmosis → guard cell turgid → decrease water potential → solute potential decreases → pressure increases K+ uptake → stoma opens
    c) Stoma closed → decrease water potential → guard cell turgid → water uptake by osmosis → K+ uptake → solute potential decreases → pressure increases → stoma opens
    d) Stoma closed → K+ uptake → solute potential decreases → decrease water potential → water uptake by osmosis → guard cell turgid → pressure increases → stoma opens
56. Quantum yield of photosynthesis decline in red light but becomes normal when it is followed by blue light. This phenomenon is known as
    a) Blackmans effect   b) Emerson effect
    c) Red drop   d) Engelmans effect

57. The number of ATP and $NADPH_2$ molecules required for the synthesis of one glucose molecule is

a) 18 and 12 b) 12 and 30

c) 12 and 18 d) 18 and 30

58. The oxidation of ethyl alcohol takes place in

a) Cytosol b) Peroxisome

c) Mitochondria d) Glyoxysome

59. The impact of air embolism is minimized in plants because of

a) Xylem are interconnected b) Presence of pit membrane

c) Both a and b d) Xylem are dead tissues

60. Which element's deficiency symptoms appear on young leaves

a) N b) Mg

c) Zn d) Mn

61. Which element's deficiency symptoms appear on older leaves

a) Ca b) Fe

c) S d) P

62. Upward movement of water is due to negative hydrostatic pressure exerted on xylem vessels. The prcssure generated due to activity of

a) Root b) Stem

c) Leaves d) Bark cells

63. In roots, maximum water absorption taken place from

a) Zone of meristematic cells

b) Zone of elongation

c) Zone of differentiation

d) All zone of roots are equally absorb water

64. Transpiration causes leaf cooling. It is due to

a) High specific heat of water

b) High heat of vaporization of water

c) High heat of fusion of water

d) High surface tension of water

65. Plants can resist certain temperature changes because they contain about 90% of water. Water will act as a thermal buffer for plant because of its

a) High specific heat b) High heat of vaporization
c) High heat of fusion d) High surface tension

66. Transpiration from leaves surface is an example of

a) Diffusion b) Osmosis
c) Imbibition d) Mass flow

67. At dynamic equilibrium during diffusion

a) Net movement of molecules is zero
b) Initially movement is slow but not zero
c) Total molecular movement is zero
d) None of these

68. Solution A has a glucose concentration of 100 mM and Solution B has a NaCl concentration of 100 mM. Both are isolated from a semipermeable membrane. Osmosis will occur from

a) A to B b) B to A
c) Osmosis not occur at all d) None of these

69. Chardakov's method for measuring water potential of plant tissue is based on

a) Density b) Pressure
c) Weight d) None of these

70. The amount of available water in soil is termed as

a) Holard b) Chesard
c) Ecahrd d) None of these

71. The amount of water which is retained by soil against gravity force is termed as

a) Field capacity b) Runoff water
c) Permanent wilting point d) None of these

72. Water movement from root hair epidermis to endodermis is

a) Apoplastic only b) Symplastic only
c) Both a and b d) None of these

73. In angiosperm's xylem tissue
   a) Only vessels are present b) Only tracheids are present
   c) Both a and b are present d) None of these

74. Transpiration is
   a) A chemical process b) A physical process
   c) A mechanical process d) Both a and c

75. Plants which are sensitive to salt condition are termed as
   a) Mesophytes b) Xerophytes
   c) Glycophytes d) Halophytes

76. Physiological drought is a condition when
   a) Soil water potential is less than plant water potential
   b) Soil water potential is greater than plant water potential
   c) Soil texture could not permit water absorption
   d) Soil structure could not permit water absorption

77. Rice tolerate water logging condition because it develop
   a) Aerenchyma tissues b) Parenchyma tissues
   c) Sclerenchyma tissues d) Pallisade cells

78. In chill sensitive plants the lipids in the membrane bilayer have
   a) High percentage of saturated fatty acids
   b) High percentage of unsaturated fatty acids
   c) Equal proportion of saturated and unsaturated fatty acids
   d) None of these

79. Select correct chemical reaction for photosynthesis
   a) $6CO_2 + 12H_2O \rightarrow C_6H_{12}O_6 + 6O_2 + 6H_2O$
   b) $6CO_2 + 6\ H_2O \rightarrow C_6H_{12}O_6 + 6O_2$
   c) $6\ CO_2 + 12H_2O \rightarrow C_6H_{12}O_6 + 6H_2O$
   d) $6CO_2 + 6\ H_2O \rightarrow C_6H_{12}O_6 + 6O_2 + 12H_2O$

80. Which of the following wall of guard cells is thick?
   a) Inner membrane b) Outer membrane
   c) Both are equally thick d) Depend on plant species

81. The hydathodes
   a) Remain closed at night
   b) Remain closed in the day
   c) Remain always open
   d) Shows specificity in opening and closing

82. Transpiration in plants will be highest when
   a) There is high humidity in the atmosphere
   b) Low wind velocity
   c) There is excess of water in the soil
   d) Environment conditions are very hot

83. Minerals are absorbed by roots plants from the soil
   a) By a process independent of water absorption
   b) Along with water absorption
   c) Only when soil solution is hypotonic to cell sap
   d) Only when the soil solution is hypertonic to the cell sap

84. Plants always take their food
   a) In inorganic form   b) In organic form
   c) In solid form   d) In soluble form

85. In plant nutrition, elements are classified as major and minor elements, depending on
   a) Their availability in the soil
   b) Their relative proportion in the ash obtained after burning the plant
   c) The relative amounts required by the plants
   d) Their relative importance in plant growth

86. Hydroponics is
   a) Studying growth of plants in soil deficient in some nutrients
   b) Studying soil conservation
   c) Growing plants in liquid culture media
   d) Growing plants under laboratory conditions

87. When the CO_2 uptake can not be increased by increasing the light, it is referred to as

a) Extinction point b) CO_2 saturation point

c) Light compensation point d) Light saturation point

88. The CO_2 compensation point is

a) Higher in C-3 plants b) Higher in C-4 plants

c) Higher in CAM plants d) Same in all plants

89. The mechanism of photosynthesis in strict chemical sense comprises

a) Two photochemical reaction

b) Two chemical reaction

c) Photochemical followed by chemical reaction

d) Chemical followed by photochemical reaction

90. In a plasmolysed cell the space between cell wall and plasma membrane is occupied by

a) External solution b) Water from cell sap

c) Both of these d) Air

91. In a flaccid cell

a) DPD = OP b) DPD = TP

c) TP = OP d) OP = 0

92. Swelling of grapes in water conforms to

a) Exosmosis b) Endosmosis

c) Diffusion d) Imbibition

93. When a cell is kept in 0.5M solution of sucrose its volume does not change. If the same cell is placed in 0.5M solution of sodium chloride, then the volume of cell will

a) Increase b) Decrease

c) Cell will be turgid d) Will not show any change

94. Root pressure is due to

a) Passive absorption b) Active absorption

c) Increase in transpiration d) Increase in phtosynthesis

95. Dixon and Jolly are associated with
   a) Light reaction of photosynthesis
   b) Anaerobic respiration
   c) Transpiration pull theory
   d) Apical dominance

96. According to cohesion theory, transport of water in plants occurs in
   a) Low pressure, low tension
   b) High pressure, high tension
   c) Low pressure, high tension
   d) High pressure, low tension

97. The common phase between aerobic and anaerobic respiration is called
   a) Tricarboxylic acid cycle
   b) Oxidative phosphorylation
   c) Embden-Myerhof-Parnas pathway
   d) Kreb cycle

98. Water enter into root hair mainly due to
   a) Turgor pressure b) Atmospheric pressure
   c) Wall pressure d) Osmotic pressure

99. Plant growth towards the light is called
   a) Photoperiodism b) Phototropism
   c) Photosyntheis d) Photolysis

100. The chilling treatment for inducing flowering in plants is known as
   a) Chilling injury b) Photomorphogenesis
   c) Vernalisation d) None of these

Answer Key of Paper-I

1.	**a**	2.	**b**	3.	**c**	4.	**b**	5.	**b**	6.	**c**	7.	**b**	8.	**b**
9.	**d**	10.	**b**	11.	**d**	12.	**c**	13.	**b**	14.	**a**	15.	**b**	16.	**c**
17.	**b**	18.	**b**	19.	**a**	20.	**c**	21.	**a**	22.	**d**	23.	**b**	24.	**c**
25.	**a**	26.	**b**	27.	**a**	28.	**b**	29.	**a**	30.	**b**	31.	**b**	32.	**a**
33.	**c**	34.	**d**	35.	**d**	36.	**c**	37.	**c**	38.	**a**	39.	**a**	40.	**d**
41.	**d**	42.	**b**	43.	**b**	44.	**c**	45.	**c**	46.	**c**	47.	**c**	48.	**c**
49.	**b**	50.	**b**	51.	**b**	52.	**b**	53.	**b**	54.	**d**	55.	**d**	56.	**b**
57.	**c**	58.	**a**	59.	**b**	60.	**d**	61.	**d**	62.	**c**	63.	**c**	64.	**b**
65.	**a**	66.	**a**	67.	**a**	68.	**a**	69.	**a**	70.	**b**	71.	**a**	72.	**c**
73.	**c**	74.	**b**	75.	**c**	76.	**a**	77.	**a**	78.	**a**	79.	**a**	80.	**a**
81.	**c**	82.	**b**	83.	**a**	84.	**a**	85.	**c**	86.	**c**	87.	**d**	88.	**a**
89.	**c**	90.	**c**	91.	**a**	92.	**b**	93.	**b**	94.	**a**	95.	**c**	96.	**c**
97.	**c**	98.	**d**	99.	**b**	100.	**c**								

PAPER-II

1. Long distance transport occurs in plants through
   a) Xylem only
   b) Phloem only
   c) Both a and b
   d) Through cell to cell
2. Which of the following is precursor of ethylene?
   a) Alanine
   b) Methionine
   c) Arginine
   d) Tryptophan
3. Which of the following is most likely to be a source?
   a) Fully mature leaves
   b) Flower
   c) Fruits
   d) New leaves
4. Naturally occurring cytokinin is/are
   a) Zeatin
   b) BAP
   c) Kinetin
   d) All of the above
5. Which of the following will increase shelf life of fruits?
   a) Ag^{++}
   b) CO_2
   c) AVG
   d) All of the above
6. Which one is an example of SDP?
   a) Cucumber
   b) Chrysanthemum
   c) Tomato
   d) Alfaalfa
7. In SDP flowering regulated by
   a) Low Pr/Pfr ratio
   b) High Pr/Pfr ratio
   c) Independent from Phytochromes
   d) None of the above
8. In plants photoperiodic signal received by
   a) Leaves
   b) Roots
   c) Bud
   d) Seeds
9. When seed develops without fertilization, the term is known as
   a) Parthenocaropy
   b) Parthenogenesis
   c) Phylogamy
   d) None

10. The plant hormone mainly responsible for cell elongation is
    a) Gibberellins b) Cytokinin
    c) Auxin d) Ethylene
11. Fruit ripening mainly caused by
    a) Gibberellins b) Cytokinin
    c) Auxin d) Ethylene
12. Natural growth hormone is
    a) NAA b) Zeatin
    c) 2,4-D d) Ethophone
13. A short day plant will flower, when provided with
    a) Longer uninterrupted dark periods
    b) Longer uninterrupted light periods
    b) Light for any duration
    d) Longer dark period with short intermittent flashes of light period
14. The photoperiodic response in plant cells is received by
    a) Chloroplast b) Phytochrome
    c) Chlorophyll d) Carotenoids
15. The essential requirement for seed germination is
    a) Water
    b) Air
    c) Water & Air
    d) Water, air and appropriate temperature
16. Leaf area index is
    a) Ratio between land area to leaf area
    b) Leaf area per unit of land area
    c) Leaf area per plant
    d) Area of single leaf

17. Phytochrome are responsible for
    a) Absoption of red and Far red light
    b) Absorption of red light
    c) Absorption of Far red light
    d) None of these
18. Phloem contents are transported from
    a) High water potential to low water potential
    b) High pressure to low pressure
    c) An area of low sugar concentration to an area of high sugar concentration
    d) From a sink to a source
19. Which of the following transport process is dependent on metabolic energy?
    a) Xylem transport b) Phloem transport
    c) Both a and b d) Both are passive process
20. Which of the following is true for companion cells?
    a) They are alive b) Present in angiosperms
    c) a is true and b is wrong d) Both a and b are true
21. In photoblastic seeds the dormancy can be broken by the treatment of
    a) Red light b) Far red light
    c) Green light d) All of the above
22. Some seeds instead of being viable, do not germinate because of
    a) Sterility b) Dormancy
    c) Parthenocarpy d) Both a and b.
23. Hard seed coat, which is prevalent in seeds of many plants results in
    a) Loss in viability
    b) Interference with water uptake
    c) Cracking of seeds
    d) None of these

24. In which form carbohydrate is translocated?
    a) Glucose b) Fructose
    c) Starch d) Sucrose
25. Which fruit will ripen in smoke?
    a) Banana b) Grape
    c) Cherry d) Orange
26. The meristem responsible for plant thickness is
    a) Apical meristem b) Lateral meristem
    c) Intercalary meristem d) None of the above
27. The growth pattern of plants and /or plant organ is
    a) C shaped b) S shaped
    c) Linear growth d) Exponential curve
28. Which of the following will increase light interception by crop canopy?
    a) Starter dose of fertilizers b) Uniform plant population
    c) High plant densities d) All of the above
29. Optimum leaf area index for any crop is the LAI where
    a) CGR is maximum
    b) Dry matter accumulation per unit of land area is maximum
    c) Both a and b
    d) Light interception is maximum
30. Which one is not true about plant hormone?
    a) Site of synthesis is differ from site of action
    b) Active in low concentration
    c) Have definite target area
    d) All have organic in nature
31. Naturally auxin was first isolated by
    a) Darwin b) Boysen-Jensen
    c) F.W. Went d) Lemark
32. Which of the following pathway synthesis auxin in plants?
    a) Indole pyruvic acid pathway
    b) Tryptamine pathway

c) Indoleacetonitrile pathway

d) All of the above

33. Not a auxin regulated response in plants

a) Flowering in pineapple

b) Parthenocarpic fruit development

c) Apical dominance

d) None of the above

34. Apical dominance is due to

a) Accumulation of auxin at apical bud

b) Accumulation of auxin at lateral buds

c) Inhibitory action of ABA synthesis by apical bud

d) Inhibitory action of ABA synthesis by lateral bud

35. During phototropism

a) Auxin accumulated at dark side

b) Auxin accumulated at illuminated side

c) Auxin equally distributed in both side

d) Auxin does not involve in phototropism

36. In gravitropism movement, root bends down wards because

a) Higher concentration of auxin at upper side increase growth

b) Higher concentration of auxin at upper side inhibit growth

c) Higher concentration of auxin at lower side inhibit growth of that side

d) Higher concentration of auxin at lower side increase growth of that side

37. Not a characteristic of auxin

a) Differentiation of xylem elements

b) Delay in abscission

c) Similar behavior for root and shoot growth

d) None of the above

38. Critical photoperiod is

a) The length of photoperiod beyond which flowering is inhibited in SDP and promoted in LDP

b) The length of photoperiod beyond which flowering is promoted in SDP and inhibited in LDP

c) Duration of light essential to perform photosynthesis

d) Minimum light period necessary for phototropism

39. Primary growth is

a) Which is initiated due to activity of apical meristem

b) Which is initiated due to activity of lateral meristem

c) Which is resulted due to activity of both apical and lateral meristem

d) None of these

40. Photosynthesis products from leaves cells to root cells are transported through

a) Xylem

b) Phloem

c) Both a and b

d) Root cells doesn't require these products

41. At maturity sieve elements retain

a) Nuclei

b) Nuclei, ribosomes

c) Nuclei, ribosomes and tonoplast

d) None of the above

42. Movement of phloem sap is

a) Only in upward direction

b) Only in downward direction

c) In both direction but in different sieve elements

d) In both direction simultaneously in same sieve elements

43. Which of the following is most likely to be a sink?
    a) Tubers
    b) Developing fruits
    c) Immature leaves
    d) All of the above

44. Phloem loading is
    a) Transfer of photosynthates from sink cells to sieve element.
    b) Transfer of photosynthates from sieve elements to sink cell.
    c) Transfer of photosynthates from source cells to sieve element.
    d) Transfer of photosynthates from sieve elements to source cell.

45. Phloem movement is pressure driven and pressure generated due to
    a) Difference in water potential at source and sink end
    b) Pressure generated due to suction force created by sink cells
    c) Differences in sieve element diameter at source and sink end
    d) Pressure generated due to source cells activity

46. Movement of solutes in phloem is an example of
    a) Diffusion
    b) Osmosis
    c) Mass flow
    d) None of the above

47. Which of the following is NOT a characteristic of plant hormone?
    a) Small organic compound
    b) Active in low concentration
    c) Regulate plant growth
    d) They usually not transported

48. Enzymes differ from plant hormones, because
    a) Active in low concentration
    b) Act within the synthesizing cells
    c) Small organic compound
    d) All of the above

49. Mulching is used to control weeds because
    a) It prevent light necessary for weed seed germination
    b) It create obstacle for water absorption by seed
    c) It increase temperature which inhibit seed germination
    d) None of these

50. Which of the following light is most effective for seed germination?
    a) Green light b) Red light
    c) Far red light d) Blue light

51. In typical monocotyledon seed, source of food material for growing embryo is
    a) Seed coat b) Endosperm
    c) Cotyledon d) Hilum

52. GA mobilizes food material in seed by inducing production of
    a) α-amylase b) β-amylase
    c) Cellulosase d) Hexokinases

53. Richmond Lang effect is
    a) Inhibition of lateral branches due to presence of auxin at apical bud
    b) Parthenocarpic fruit development through application of auxin
    c) Increase in plant height due to application of GA
    d) Delay in senescence due to application of cytokinin

54. The removal of apical bud will ———— branching
    a) Increase b) Decrease
    c) Maintain d) Not affect

55. GA induce flowering in
    a) Short day plants b) Long day plants
    c) Day natural plants d) None of these

56. Secondary growth of plant means that a plant grows
    a) A second time b) Increase in girth
    c) Increase in height d) Towards light

57. Plants grow in size because of
    a) Addition of cells b) Increase in size of cells
    c) Enlargement of cells d) Elongation of cells

58. The rate of plant growth can be measured by
    a) Manometer b) Auxanometer
    c) Photometer d) Porometer

59. The germination of bean seed is said to be epigeal because
    a) The leaves are born outside the soil
    b) The root do not come out of the soil
    c) The cotyledons are brought out of soil
    d) The roots come out of the soil

60. The radicle of the seedling always grows
    a) Towards gravity b) Away from gravity
    c) Neutral to gravity d) Towards light

61. The part that germinate and grows first in seed is
    a) Plumule b) Radicle
    c) Cotyledons d) Epicotyl

62. The plants will stop growing if the shoot tip is cut off because
    a) Shoot tip produce growth hormones
    b) Shoot tip contain meristematic cells
    c) Shoot tip is growing part
    d) The plant will lose water

63. Growth in higher plants takes place
    a) By the growing points scattered all over the plant body
    b) By the growing points confined to certain region
    c) In the entire plant body
    d) In aerial parts only

64. Chemical substances that have effect on growth of plants are called
    a) Enzymes b) Catalyst
    c) Hormones d) Pesticides

65. Temperature treatment which shortens the vegetative period and hastens flowering is called

a) Phototropism b) Photoperiodism

c) Vernalisation d) Thermoregulation

66. Which of the following is responsible for geotropic responses in plants?

a) Abcisic acid b) Gibbrellins

c) Auxin d) Cytokinin

67. The hormone which stimulates the flowering in vernalized plant is

a) Florigen b) Vernalin

c) Cytokinin c) Gibberellin

68. In which of the following stage, rate of growth gradually slow down and comes to steady state

a) Lag phase b) Log phase

c) Exponential stage d) Stationary stage

69. Stratification is a method of overcoming dormancy in seeds which

a) Contain immature embryo

b) Hard seed coat

c) Contain fully formed but physiological unripe embryo

d) Presence of any inhibitor chemical

70. Which of the following growth hormone in plants is influenced by light

a) Gibbrellins b) Cytokinin

c) Auxin d) Ethylene

71. Which of the following affects fruit setting in plants?

a) Self incompatibility b) Stigma receptibility

c) Pollinating agent d) All of the above

72. ——— is/are climacteric fruit/s.

a) Citrus b) Grape

c) Mango d) All of the above.

73. ——— is/are non climacteric fruit/s.

a) Apple b) Banana

c) Pineapple d) All of the above

74. Which one is not true for abscission?

a) Auxin reduces sensitivity of abscission zone cells to ethylene.

b) Auxin increase sensitivity of abscission zone cells to ethylene.

c) Auxin and ethylene interaction cause abscission of leaves.

d) Higher level of auxin prevents formation of abscission layer.

75. Which is a plant hormone?

a) CH_3-CH_3 b) CH_2=CH_2

c) Both a and b d) None of the above

76. Monocarpic plants are

a) Plants which flower only once in their life period.

b) Plants which flowers retain only one carpel.

c) Plants which bear only one flower in their life cycle.

d) None of the above.

77. Which of the following sentence is NOT true for plant growth?

a) Plant growth occurs in specialized tissue only.

b) Plant growth occurs evenly in every tissues of plant.

c) In plant growth always size or volume will increase.

d) In plant growth not always dry weight will increase.

78. Increase in plant girth is result of

a) Apical meristem activity

b) Lateral meristem activity

c) Intercalary meristem

d) It is combined effect of all three meristem.

79. In a hypothetical situation, wheat variety was grown in a field which was surrounded by Mango trees. Farmer noticed that wheat yield was normal from middle of the field while there was large yield reduction from border rows. The probable reason is
    a) Border row plants compete for water and other nutrients with mango tree.
    b) Canopy photosynthesis may limit in border rows.
    c) Border rows wheat doesn't meet their photoperiodic requirement.
    d) It may be due to pest/disease attack from mango trees.
80. Food made at a source is translocated to nearby sinks, often on the same side of the plant. Why does this happen?
    a) The food is used by the plant before it reaches distant sinks.
    b) The starch in the phloem cannot travel rapidly and never reaches distant sinks
    c) Vascular tissue in the leaf and stem is organized into discrete bundles, which run the length of the organ.
    d) Sieve tube elements contain recognition compounds, which prevent food from distant sources from entering them.
81. Which statement best describes the movement of food through the phloem?
    a) From immature leaves to roots
    b) From roots and seeds to mature leaves
    c) From mature leaves to roots and seeds
    d) From immature leaves to mature leaves
82. Based on Münch's pressure-flow hypothesis, which of the following conditions would increase the rate of translocation?
    a) A decrease in photosynthesis
    b) A decrease in phloem unloading at the sink
    c) An increase in sucrose production at the source
    d) An increase in the humidity in the outside air

83. What is endosperm?
    a) Male reproductive cells in plants
    b) Stored food in seed
    c) Cell that make pollen grain
    d) Fleshy part of the fruit
84. The abscission layer
    a) Causes a shoot tip to bend towards light
    b) Secrete cytokinin
    c) The location of biological clock
    d) Where a leaf separates from a stem
85. Most plants flower when
    a) The soil reaches a certain temperature
    b) The day are of right length
    c) A certain number of of days have passed since they last flowered
    d) The night are of right length
86. What is a tropism?
    a) An internal chemical signal that controls a plant's growth and development
    b) A movement in response to an external stimulus
    c) A movement in response to light stimulus
    d) A pigment that absorbs light and affects seed germination
87. What is phytochrome?
    a) A pigment that absorbs light and affects photosynthesis
    b) A pigment that absorbs light and affects seed germination
    c) A pigment that sense gravity and affects seed germination
    d) A macronutrient
88. How would gibberellic acid be beneficial to plants?
    a) By suppressing lateral buds, the plant will not have too many leaves to block each other's availability to light.
    b) By hastening the ripening of fruit, the plant's seeds will be dispersed sooner

c) By promoting leaf senescence, the plant can save energy by reabsorbing photosynthetically important moleculcs.

d) By increasing stem and internode elongation, the plant will be able to grow taller and gain access to light.

89. What is a major function of auxin?

a) Controls the abscission of leaves

b) Promotes stem elongation

c) Absorbs light and affects seed germination

d) Component of proteins

90. How would phototropism be beneficial to plants?

a) By keeping the leaves oriented perpendicularly to light, the plant can increase water loss.

b) By keeping the leaves oriented parallel to light, the plant can increase water loss.

c) By keeping the leaves oriented perpendicularly to light, the plant can increase the photosynthesis rate.

d) By keeping the leaves oriented parallel to light, the plant can decrease the photosynthesis rate.

91. Arrange the following five events in an order that explains the mass flow of materials in the phloem.

1. Water diffuses into the sieve elements.
2. Leaf cells produce sugar by photosynthesis.
3. Solutes are actively transported into sieve elements.
4. Sugar is transported from cell to cell in the leaf.
5. Sugar moves down the stem.

a) 2, 1, 4, 3, 5 b) 2,4,1,5,3

c) 2, 4, 3, 1, 5 d) 2, 4, 1, 3, 5

92. Arrange the following six events in correct order that explain flowering in plants:

1. Transition factors (i.e. size, age)
2. Juvenile vegetative stage
3. Adult vegetative phase
4. Adult reproductive stage

5. Environmental factors (photoperiod, tempreature)
6. Flowering

a) 1, 2,3,4,5,6 b) 2,3,1,4,5,6
c) 2, 1, 3,5,4,6 d) 2, 3, 4,1,5,6

93. When GA induced tall plant is crossed with pure tall plant, phenotypic ratio of F2 generation is likely to be

a) All tall b) 50% tall and 50% dwarf
c) 75% tall and 25% dwarf d) All dwarf

94. Dwarfness of the plant can be controlled by treating it with

a) GA b) IAA
c) C_2H_2 d) BAP

95. Gibberellins are characterised by

a) Increasing amylase activity
b) Removal of genetic dwarfism
c) Induction of flowering in LDP
d) All of these

96. Delay of senescence is characteristics of?

a) IAA b) GA
c) Cytokinin d) ABA

97. A naturally occurring growth inhibitor is

a) IAA b) GA
c) Cytokinin d) ABA

98. Most plants show change over from vegetative to reproductive stage in response to

a) Increase in temperature b) Change in day length
c) Oxygen present in the air d) Food material available

Answer Key of Paper-II

1.	**c**	2.	**b**	3.	**a**	4.	**a**	5.	**d**	6.	**b**	7.	**b**	8.	**a**
9.	**a**	10.	**c**	11.	**d**	12.	**b**	13.	**a**	14.	**b**	15.	**d**	16.	**b**
17.	**a**	18.	**b**	19.	**b**	20.	**d**	21.	**a**	22.	**b**	23.	**b**	24.	**d**
25.	**a**	26.	**b**	27.	**b**	28.	**d**	29.	**c**	30.	**c**	31.	**c**	32.	**d**
33.	**d**	34.	**a**	35.	**a**	36.	**c**	37.	**c**	38.	**a**	39.	**a**	40.	**b**
41.	**d**	42.	**c**	43.	**d**	44.	**c**	45.	**a**	46.	**c**	47.	**d**	48.	**b**
49.	**a**	50.	**b**	51.	**b**	52.	**a**	53.	**d**	54.	**a**	55.	**b**	56.	**b**
57.	**d**	58.	**b**	59.	**c**	60.	**a**	61.	**b**	62.	**b**	63.	**b**	64.	**c**
65.	**c**	66.	**c**	67.	**b**	68.	**d**	69.	**c**	70.	**c**	71.	**d**	72.	**c**
73.	**c**	74.	**b**	75.	**b**	76.	**b**	77.	**b**	78.	**b**	79.	**b**	80.	**c**
81.	**c**	82.	**c**	83.	**b**	84.	**d**	85.	**d**	86.	**b**	87.	**b**	88.	**b**
89.	**a**	90.	**c**	91.	**c**	92.	**c**	93.	**c**	94.	**a**	95.	**d**	96.	**c**
97.	**d**	98.	**b**												

PAPER-III

1. Increase in length of plant axis is caused by
   a) Cork cambium
   b) Vascular cambium
   c) Apical meristem
   d) Mitotic division in pith and cortex
2. Meristematic cells are
   a) Differentiated cell
   b) Dedifferentiated cells
   c) Mature and living
   d) Immature and living
3. Which process is not involved in the development of seed into a mature plant
   a) Mitosis
   b) Differentiation of cells
   c) Meiosis
   d) Increase in size of cellls
4. If the seedling are grown in darkness
   a) They are similar to those grown in light
   b) They are taller than those grown in light
   c) They are of same size as those grown in light
   d) They are much healthier than those grown in light
5. The dry weight accumulated per unit of plant dry weight, per unit of time is called as
   a) RGR
   b) CGR
   c) NAR
   d) Biomass
6. Biological clock is set in plant when it is exposed to
   a) CO_2 enviornment
   b) Light
   c) Low temperature
   d) UV radiation
7. Hormone differ from enzymes in that
   a) Hormones are found only in animals
   b) Hormones are found only in plants
   c) Hormones are completely used up during metabolism
   d) Hormones are not used up at all in the metabolism

8. Fruit drop is caused by
   a) Less auxin in fruit than stem
   b) More auxin in fruit than in stem
   c) Equal distribution of auxin in stem and fruit
   d) Absence of auxin in stem and fruit
9. Highest concentration of auxin found
   a) At the base of various plant organ
   b) In leaves
   c) In growing tips
   d) In xylem and phloem only
10. Negative geotropism in horizontal stem is caused by
   a) Accumulation of auxin at lower side
   b) Accumulation of auxin at upper side
   c) Cell shrinkage on the lower side
   d) Cell enlargement on the upper side
11. IAA generally inhibits the growth of
   a) Roots b) Shoots
   c) Leaves d) Plants in general
12. Apical dominance in plants is due to
   a) Auxin only
   b) Cytokinin only
   c) Balance action of auxin and cytokinin
   d) None of these
13. Gibberellins has been successfully employed to induce flowering in
   a) Short day plants under long day condition
   b) Long day plants under short day conditions
   c) Day neutral plants
   d) Few plant species

14. Which of the following is not a natural auxin

a) Indole-3-actonitrile b) Indole-3-acetaldehyde

c) Indole-3-ethanol d) Indole-3-butyric acid

15. The enzyme nitrilase converts

a) Indole acetonitrile to IAA b) IAA to Indole acetonitrile

c) Indole pyruvic acid to IAA d) Tryptamine to IAA

16. Which form of ABA is biologically most active

a) ABA^+ in cis - form b) ABA^+ in trans – form

c) ABA^- in cis - form d) ABA^- in trans – form

17. The site of synthesis and site of action of florigen is

a) Root and leaves respectively

b) Root and shoot tip respectively

c) Shoot tip and leaf respectively

d) Leaf and shoot tip respectively

18. Which of the following extend shelf life of fruits but not affecting ethylene biosynthesis

a) STS b) $AgNO_3$

c) $KMnO_4$ d) AVG

19. RGR of any plant will ——— with age

a) Increase b) Decrease

c) Not change d) Depend on plant species

20. If a short day plant is given 8 hour light and 16 hours dark and the dark period is interrupted by a flash of 730 nm wavelength in the middle, then

a) The plant remains vegetative

b) The plant produce flowers

c) The plant produces 1 or 2 flowers only

d) The floral apex dies

21. If a plant produces flowers on exposure to alternating exposure of 4 hours light and 2 hours dark in a 24 hour cycle, it should be

    a) Short day plant b) Short long day plant

    c) Long short day plant d) Long day plant

22. If a long day plant is given 8 hours light and 16 hours dark and the dark period is interrupted by two flashes in the middle- a flash of 730 nm followed by another flash of 660 nm

    a) The plant remains vegetative

    b) The plant produce flowers

    c) The floral apex is scorched

    d) The plant produces a few sterile plant

23. It is thought that phytochrome are located

    a) In side the chloroplast

    b) In side the vacuole

    c) On the nuclear envelope

    d) Within the plasma membrane

24. The site of vernalization is

    a) Cotyledon b) Root apex

    c) Shoot apex d) Flower bud

25. Cell organelle found only in plants is

    a) Mitochondria b) Golgi complex

    c) Ribosomes d) Plastids

26. One of the following is a precursor of auxin

    a) Phenylalanine b) Methionine

    c) Tryptophan d) Cystine

27. Phytochrome involved in

    a) Seed germination b) Flowering

    c) Shade avoidance d) All of these

28. Stomatal closure in response to water stress is mediated by

a) IAA b) GA

c) Ethylene d) ABA

29. A degraded sample of yeast DNA contains

a) GA b) Cytokinin

c) ABA d) Ethylene

30. Which of the following is not known from the plants

a) Kinetin b) Zeatin

c) Ribosylzeatin d) 2 ip

31. Shoot differentiation in callus can be induced by a combination of

a) Low auxin and high cytokinin

b) High auxin and low cytokinin

c) Equal proportion of auxin and cytokinin

d) Only cytokinin and no auxin

32. The precursor of ABA is

a) Kaurene b) Tryptophan

c) Glucobrassin d) Carotenoid

33. Photomorphogenetic pigment in plant is

a) Chlorophyll b) Xanthophyll

c) Phytochrome d) Carotene

34. It is believed that florigen comprises

a) GA and Auxin b) GA and cytokinin

c) GA and anthesin d) GA and vernelin

35. Cholodny-Went theory successfully explains

a) Photorespiration b) Phtomorphogenesis

c) Phototropism d) Photoperiodism

36. Which of the following is correctly describe events necessary for flowering in plants

 a) Juvenile vegetative phase> transition factors (i.e., size, age) > induce hormonal or other changes > adult vegetative phase > environmental signal (i.e., photoperiod, temperature) > adult reproductive phase >flowering expressed

 b) Juvenile vegetative phase > adult vegetative phase > adult reproductive phase > flowering

 c) Juvenile vegetative phase > transition factors (*i.e.*, size, age) > induce hormonal or other changes > adult vegetative phase > adult reproductive phase > flowering

 d) Flowering is regulated by plants genetic constituents and independent from environments

37. Plant development is highly plastic, it means

 a) Ability of plant to change form or shape in response to environment with heritable changes

 b) Ability of plant to change form or shape in response to environment without any heritable changes

 c) Plant could not change its shape or form in response to environment

 d) Plant develop solid woody body

38. Arrange the correct sequence of plant embryogenesis stages

 1. Proembryo 2. Heart shaped 3. Torpedo 4. Globular

 a) 1,2, 3, 4 b) 1, 4, 3, 2

 c) 1, 4, 2, 3 d) 1, 3,2, 4

39. Select best explanation for that why not any IAA synthesis mutant is discovered

 a) IAA involve in many vital process

 b) There are more than one biosynthesis pathways for auxin

 c) There may be mutant but are not viable so are not detected in genetic screens

 d) All of these

40. More than 125 GAs are known and numbers are still increasing. They are designated as GA_1,—— GA_{125}. The number indicated

a) The position of –OH group and number of carbon atoms

b) The position of –OH, -COOH and –CH_3 group on C20 of gibberellin ring

c) The position of –OH, -COOH and –CH_3 group on C19 of gibberellin ring

d) The number indicate only sequence of their discovery

41. The level of ———— plant hormone increases during flooding

a) Auxin
b) Cytokinin
c) Ethylene
d) ABA

42. Arrange the correct sequence of ethylene biosynthesis

1. Methionine
2. 1, Aminocyclopropane-1-caroxylic acid (ACC)
3. S- Adenosyl-L- Methinine (SAM)
4. Ethylene

a) 1, 2, 3,4
b) 2, 3, 1, 4
c) 1,3,2, 4
d) 3, 2, 1,4

43. PHY A and phy A indicate about

a) Appoprotein and Holoprotein of phytochrome A

b) Holoprotein and apoprotein of phyochrome A

c) Wild type and mutant gene of phytochrome A

d) Mutant gene and wild type of phytochrome A

44. Which of the following structures is not used in eukaryotic protein manufacture and secretion?

a) Ribosome
b) Rough ER
c) Golgi complex
d) Lysosomes

45. Starch grains in the potato tuber are located in

a) Chloroplasts
b) Leucoplasts
c) Chromoplasts
d) Elioplasts

46. When the growth of a plant or organ remains arrested due to internal factors, the phenomenon precisely termed as

a) Quiescence b) Imposed dormancy

c) Innate dormancy d) Dormancy

47. Seeds whose germination is inhibited by light are called as

a) Photophobic b) Photoblastic

c) Negatively photophobic d) Negatively photoblastic

48. The term statolith is applied to

a) Large starch grain

b) Fragments of ER

c) Cell containing starch grain

d) Cell containing fragments of ER

49. ————— increase membrane bound proton pump

a) GA b) Auxin

c) Ethylene d) ABA

50. A section of root grow only in length but not in thickness, the cell division may be

a) Anticlinal only

b) Periclinal only

c) Initially periclinal and later anticlinal

d) Initially periclinal than anticlinal

51. Plant density of a crop is 50,000 plant ha^{-1}. Initially leaf area of 20 plants is 40,000 cm^2. What will be the LAI at this stage

a) 1 b) 2000

c) 0.1 d) 20

52. Phytochrome has molecular weight of

a) 100 kda b) 110 kda

c) 120 kda d) 130 kda

53. Phytochrome is
    a) Lipoprotein-pigment complex
    b) Lipid pigment complex
    c) Carbohydrate-pigment complex
    d) Glycoprotein-pigment complex
54. A characteristic feature of ripening of some fruits is sudden increase in respiration which is known as
    a) Anthesis b) Photorespiration
    c) Climacteric d) Climatic
55. A natural growth regulator is
    a) Benzyaldehyde b) 2,4 D
    c) NAA d) Ethylene
56. GA differ from auxin since they produce
    a) Cell division b) Stem elongation
    c) Root initiation d) Shortening of internode
57. What is NOT true for light and plant relationship
    a) Light is essential for photosynthesis
    b) Light regulated plant architecture
    c) Action spectra for photosynthesis and photo morphogenesis are nearly similar
    d) Absorption spectra for photosynthesis and photo morphogenesis are similar
58. What does the term developmental plasticity mean?
    a) Individuals can adapt to their environment and become new species
    b) Completely unrelated species can closely resemble one another over time.
    c) There is natural variation in a population
    d) This is the tendency for genetically identical individuals to differ in response to environmental stimuli

59. Which of the following would not have an effect on flowering of a particular plant species?

   a) Nutritional status b) Prevailing winds

   c) Temperature d) Plant age

60. The plant pigment phytochrome is able to switch between sensing red light and sensing far-red light because

   a) Phytochrome can sense all wavelengths of visible light.

   b) It is a protein that can alternate between two conformations

   c) Phytochrome is the name for a group of pigments which each sense a particular color of light.

   d) It is composed of two separate light-sensing areas

61. There are two widely accepted theories on how roots sense gravity. One theory states that amyloplasts in the root cap settle to the bottom of the cells and exert pressure downward. What is the name of this theory?

   a) The gravitational pressure hypothesis

   b) The amyloplast hypothesis

   c) The root cell hypothesis

   d) The statolith hypothesis

62. The important finding in Went's experiment was

   a) The curvature of coleoptile was proportional to the concentration of auxins

   b) The presence of elongation promoting substance in all cells of root.

   c) The curvature in few coleoptiles was due to irregular elongation of cells

   d) That there is unequal distribution of elongation promoting substance in Avena coleoptile

63. Plant growth hormones extracted from a fungus and a fish are respectively

   a) Auxins and 2, 4-D b) Ethylene and cytokinin

   c) Gibberellin and kinetin d) Gibberellin and zeatin

64. In plants IAA causes cell elongation due to
    a) Increase in pH of Apoplast
    b) Increase in pH of cytoplasm
    c) Decrease in pH of Apoplast
    d) Increase in pH of cytoplasm
65. Short Day plants flowers when
    a) Night > critical dark period
    b) Dark period interrupted by flash of light
    c) Night < critical dark period
    d) Night < critical dark period & day length is interrupted by dark period
66. The term alternation of generations refers to a plant's life cycle alternating between
    a) The production of haploid gametes by meiosis with the production of diploid spores by mitosis.
    b) A haploid gametophyte generation and a haploid sporophyte generation.
    c) A haploid gametophyte generation and a diploid sporophyte generation
    d) A flower producing generation and a leaf-producing generation
67. When a plant structure such as a leaf is injured, it produces _______, which may cause the part to age and drop off
    a) Cytokinin   b) Ethylene
    c) Auxins   d) Abscisic acid
68. In the autumn, the amount of _____ increases and the amount of _____ decreases in fruit and leaf stalks, causing a plant to drop fruit and leaves
    a) Ethylene . . . auxin
    b) Gibberellin . . . abscisic acid
    c) Cytokinin . . . abscisic acid
    d) Auxin . . . ethylene

69. In contrast to animals, plants exhibit ______ and _____

    a) Determinate growth . . . persistent morphogenesis

    b) Indeterminate growth . . . are not capable of morphogenesis throughout their lifespan

    c) Indeterminate growth . . . persistent morphogenesis

    d) Indeterminate growth . . . cellular differentiation

70. Which of the following seedlings will probably bend toward the light?

    a) Tip covered with a cap made of black plastic

    b) Tip cut off and place a block of agar over half of the cut portion; the side with the agar block will bend towards the light

    c) Tip cut off

    d) Tip separated from base by a gelatin block

71. In shoots, branching is inhibited by _____ from the tip of a growing shoot, but this effect is countered by _____ from the roots.

    a) Cytokinins . . . auxins   b) Gibberellins . . . ethylene

    c) Auxins . . . cytokinins   d) Auxins . . . abscisic acid

72. A biological cycle with a period of about 24 hours is called

    a) Thigmotropism   b) A circadian rhythm

    c) Photoperiod   d) A biological clock

73. _______ appear to be responsible for gravitropism

    a) Statoliths   b) Phytoalexins

    c) Gibberellins   d) Phytochromes

74. A certain short-day plant flowers when days are less than 12 hours long. Which of the following would cause it to flower?

    a) A 9-hour night and 15-hour day with 1 minute of darkness after 7 hour

    b) An 8-hr day and 16-hour night with a flash of white light after 8 hr.

c) A 13-hour night and 11-hour day with 1 minute of darkness after 6 hr.

d) A 12-hour day and 12-hour night with a flash of red light after 6 hr.

75. A chemical change in a substance called phytochrome

a) Causes a plant to bend toward light

b) Triggers fruit drop

c) Enables a plant to respond to the presence of light.

d) Allows a plant to deal with stresses like shortage of water.

76. Cytokinin synthesis is maximum in

a) Roots b) Leaves

c) Shoots tip d) Fruits

77. In India most of plant flowers during spring or summer because

a) It is breeding season for butterflies

b) More solar radiation are available

c) Fruit and seed setting must be complete before onset of monsoon

d) Environmental fluctuations are low

78. Phytohormone responsible for conversion of stored proteins into glucose in germinating cereals is

a) Cytokinin b) Auxin

c) Gibberellin d) Abscissic Acid

79. The phytohormone which provides desiccation resistance to embryo in germinating seed is

a) Gibberellic acid b) Ethylene

c) Abssicic acid d) Cytokinin

80. One of the followings is an example of ABA-insensitive systems

a) Vivipary b) Bud dormancy

c) Seed dormancy d) None of these

81. Plant hormones act by affecting the activities of
    a) Genes
    b) Membranes
    c) Genes, membranes, and enzymes.
    d) Genes and enzymes
82. Which of the following associated with crown gall disease caused by *Agrobacterium*
    a) Auxin and GA
    b) Auxin and cytokinin
    c) Cytokinin and GA
    d) Cytokinin only
83. AMO 1618 is inhibitor of
    a) Auxin
    b) GA
    c) Cytokinin
    d) Etylene
84. By which technique you can evaluate polar transport of phytohormones
    a) ELISA
    b) Radio Immuno Assays (RIA)
    c) HPLC
    d) Donar receiver agar block
85. Auxin stimulate cell elongation by
    a) Increasing turgour pressure
    b) Increasing wall extensibility
    c) Synthesis of new wall material
    d) All of these
86. TIBA act as anti auxin by
    a) Inhibiting auxin biosynthesis
    b) Reduce free auxin pool
    c) Inhibiting translocation of auxin
    d) All of these

87. ———— will reduce apical dominance in intact plant

a) Auxin b) GA

c) Cytokinin d) Etylene

88. US army use a chemical coded as agent orange during Vietnam war, it was

a) Mixture of 2,4-D and 2,4,5 T

b) Only 2,4-D

c) Only 2,4-T

d) ABA

89. Which of the following is not a phytochrome regulated response

a) Seed germination

b) Formation of leaf primordia

c) Stomatal movement

d) Anthocynin production

90. ABC gene model explain development of floral whorl. According to this

a) Activity of A responsible for petals, A-B for sepals, B-C for stamens and C for carpel

b) Activity of A responsible for sepals, A-B for petals, B-C for stamens and C for carpel

c) Activity of A responsible for sepals, A-B for petals, B-C for carpel and C for stamens

d) Activity of A responsible for petals, A-B for sepals, B-C for carpel and C for stamens

91. GA mobilizes food material during seed germination by inducing synthesis of α-amylase. GA and α-amylase synthesized in

a) GA and α-amylase synthesized by Embryo

b) GA and α-amylase synthesized by aleurone layer

c) GA synthesized by embryo and α-amylase by aleurone layer

d) GA synthesized by aleurone layer and α-amylase by embryo

92. Translocation of food material to embryo through mother plant is
    a) Apoplastic only
    b) Symplastic only
    c) Both a and b
    d) No translocation from mother plant.

93. Epigeal germination occurs due to
    a) Higher growth of epicotyl region
    b) Higher growth of hypocotyl region
    c) When both regions cells equally enlarge and divide
    d) None of these

94. "FlavrSavr" is a transgenic tomato. Which have
    a) Antisense mRNA of ACC synthetase
    b) Antisense mRNA of ACC oxidase
    b) Antisense mRNA of Both gene
    d) None of these

95. CGR (Crop grwoth rate) depends on leaf area of plant. Select correct relationship
    a) CGR = NAR/LAI
    b) CGR = LAI/NAR
    c) CGR = NAR x LAI
    d) CGR is independent from NAR

Answer Key of Paper-III

1.	**c**	2.	**d**	3.	**c**	4.	**b**	5.	**a**	6.	**b**	7.	**c**	8.	**a**
9.	**c**	10.	**a**	11.	**a**	12.	**c**	13.	**b**	14.	**d**	15.	**a**	16.	**c**
17.	**d**	18.	**c**	19.	**b**	20.	**b**	21.	**d**	22.	**a**	23.	**d**	24.	**c**
25.	**d**	26.	**c**	27.	**d**	28.	**d**	29.	**b**	30.	**a**	31.	**a**	32.	**d**
33.	**c**	34.	**c**	35.	**c**	36.	**a**	37.	**b**	38.	**c**	39.	**d**	40.	**d**
41.	c	42.	c	43.	b	44.	d	45.	d	46.	c	47.	d	48.	c
49.	**b**	50.	**a**	51.	**a**	52.	**c**	53.	**c**	54.	**c**	55.	**d**	56.	**b**
57.	**c**	58.	**d**	59.	**b**	60.	**b**	61.	**d**	62.	**a**	63.	**c**	64.	**c**
65.	**a**	66.	**c**	67.	**b**	68.	**a**	69.	**c**	70.	**d**	71.	**c**	72.	**b**
73.	**a**	74.	**c**	75.	**c**	76.	**a**	77.	**c**	78.	**c**	79.	**c**	80.	**a**
81.	**c**	82.	**b**	83.	**b**	84.	**d**	85.	**b**	86.	**c**	87.	**c**	88.	**a**
89.	**d**	90.	**b**	91.	**c**	92.	**a**	93.	**b**	94.	**a**	95.	**c**		

PAPER-IV

1. Choose the correct statement
   a) Etiolation is irreversible
   b) Etiolation and albinism are the same
   c) Albinism is genetical while etiolation is physiological
   d) Etiolation is genetical
2. A certain short-day plant flowers when days are less than 12 hours long. Which of the following would cause it to flower?
   a) 9-hour night and 15-hour day with 1 minute of darkness after 7 hour.
   b) 8-hr day and 16-hour night with a flash of white light after 8 hr.
   c) 13-hour night and 11-hour day with 1 minute of darkness after 6 hr.
   d) 12-hour day and 12-hour night with a flash of red light after 6 hr.
3. Radiation below about 700 nm will activate photoconversion of
   a) Pr b) Pfr
   c) Both Pr and Pfr d) None
4. An advantage of an open canopied variety of any crop with upper right leaves as compared to a closed variety with horizontal leaves would be:
   a) Smaller light would be intercepted
   b) Square inch of the top leaves has higher photosynthetic rates
   c) Light penetrates deeper into the crop canopy
   d) Light does not penetrate as deeply into the crop canopy
5. Two hypothetical genetically similar mango trees are grown in two different climatic zones (Zone A and Zone B). These zones

differ from each other only in diurnal temperature and in zone A average night temperature is more as compared to zone B). Other parameters like sunshine hours, wind velocity, soil fertility, average day temperature and relative humidity are remain same in these two climatic zones. Which is true about the difference in biomass between the two trees?

a) Tree which grown in zone A acquire higher biomass

b) Tree which grown in zone B acquire higher biomass

c) There is no difference for biomass.

d) We can't predict anything from this information

6. Food made at a source is translocated to nearby sinks, often on the same side of the plant. Why does this happen?

a) The food is used by the plant before it reaches distant sinks.

b) The starch in the phloem cannot travel rapidly and never reaches distant sinks

c) Vascular tissue in the leaf and stem is organized into discrete bundles, which run the length of the organ.

d) Sieve tube elements contain recognition compounds, which prevent food from distant sources from entering them.

7. Why is the root apical meristem covered by a thimble-shaped cap, while the shoot apical meristem is not?

a) The root cap senses gravity, and shoot apical meristems do not need to sense gravity.

b) In order to respire, the shoot apical meristem cannot be covered.

c) Roots seek out water, while shoots do not

d) Roots need protection as they grow through the soil.

8. Which of the following gives the correct sequence of events during germination?

a) Water uptake, protein synthesis, increased oxygen consumption, mRNA synthesis, radicle emergence

b) Radicle emergence, water uptake, increased oxygen consumption, protein synthesis, mRNA synthesis

c) mRNA synthesis, protein synthesis, water uptake, increased oxygen consumption, radicle emergence

d) Water uptake, increased oxygen consumption, protein synthesis, mRNA synthesis, radicle emergence

9. Global warming affects plant growth by :

a) Extending maturity period

b) Decreasing maturity period

c) Maturity delay with slow growth

c) Growth and development in plant is genetically regulated.

10. There are two varieties of any hypothetical crop-determinate and indeterminate type. Which one type variety will perform well in the area where dry spell in crop season are most frequent:

a) Determinate growth habit

b) Indeterminate growth habit

c) Both have same performance

d) None of these

11. Which one physiological activity first affected by moisture stress:

a) Photosynthesis b) Cell Elongation

c) Cell division d) Cell differentiation

Answer Key of Paper IV

1. **c** 2. **c** 3. a 4. **c** 5. **b** 6. **a** 7. **d** 8. **b**

9. **b** 10. **b** 11. **b**

PAPER-V

1. Two broadleaf trees are growing side by side on a hot summer day. One has leaves that are light-colored and reflective of sunlight; the other has dark green leaves. The tree with light-colored leaves has cooler leaf temperatures, but otherwise everything about the trees is identical (same leaf shape, same stomatal conductance, same sun exposure, same wind, etc). Which is true about the difference in transpiration rates between the two trees?
   a) Higher transpiration for tree with light colored leaves
   b) Lower transpiration for tree with light colored leaves
   c) We can't predict anything about transpiration from this information.
   d) Depends on soil water availability
2. Quantum flux is represented as
   a) μmol photon m^{-2} s^{-1} b) μmol quanta m^{-2} s^{-1}
   c) J $m^{-2}s^{-1}$ d) W $m^{-2}s^{-1}$
3. Which of the following is not a characteristic of shade plants?
   a) Low Leaf area ratio
   b) Low root : shoot ratio
   c) Low light compensation point
   d) None of the above
4. Which of the following is NOT true for excurrent tree?
   a) Stem terminal end grow faster as compared to lateral branches
   b) Mostly these are pines and other gymnosperm
   c) Broad crown form present in these trees
   d) None of these
5. Which of the following is true for crown form of tropical trees?
   a) When they young they have long tapering
   b) When they adult they have rounded crown

c) At maturity their crown become flat

d) All of the above

6. In a tropical mesic sites tree develops

a) Short leaves with small crown

b) Short leaves with large crown

c) Tall with broad crown

d) Small and narrow crown

7. In a tropical xeric condition tree develops

a) Short leaves with small crown

b) Short leaves with large crown

c) Tall with broad crown

d) Small and narrow crown

8. Primary productivity is

a) Accumulated biomass of autotrophs

b) Accumulated biomass of herbivores

c) Accumulated biomass of heterotrophs

d) Accumulated biomass of an ecosystem

9. Pigments absorb light of different wavelengths, such as blue light (425-490 nm) and red light (640-700 nm). If a single photon of blue light and red light are each absorbed and passed to the reaction center, which photon will provide the most energy for use in photosynthesis?

a) Blue light

b) Red light

c) Both have same energy photons

d) None of the above

10. Shade tolerant species have low light compensation point because of

a) Higher photosynthetic rate b) Higher respiration rate

c) Lower photosynthetic rate d) Lower respiration rate

11. Two hypothetical tree species have same crown features and same photosynthetic rate. Tree A having higher rate of respiration as compared to tree B) At low light levels which is true for difference in net primary productivity of two trees?

    a) Tree A gave higher NPP

    b) Tree B gave higher NPP

    c) Both have same NPP

    d) We can't predict anything from this information

12. Which of the following adaptation not increase light interception by lower strata canopy?

    a) Horizontal leaf inclination

    b) More chlorophyll per unit of leaf area

    c) Higher specific leaf area

    d) Higher respiration rate

13. Which of the following adaptation will increase gas exchange within the canopy?

    a) Amount of chlorophyll per unit of leaf area

    b) Loose packing of leaves in vertical space

    c) Leaf density

    d) Both b and c

14. The given figure indicate rate of photosynthesis at different irradiance level. Observe the given figure and answer the following questions.

    1. The rate of photosynthesis in the region of the curve labeled "A" is determined by:

    a) The amount of light striking the leaf

    b) The rate of the light-independent reactions

    c) The rate of the light-dependent reactions

    d) Answers A and C are correct

2. Which one of the following statements correctly describes photosynthesis at light levels at or above level "B"?

a) The overall rate of photosynthesis is limited by the amount of CO_2 available.

b) Photosynthesis has stopped and O_2 is no longer being produced.

c) The amount of light is limiting the rate of photosynthesis.

d) The light-dependent reactions are operating at the maximum rate.

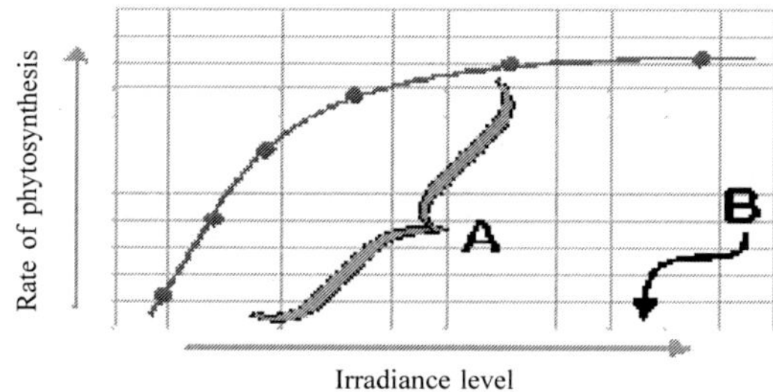

15. The function of stomata is to

a) Regulate movements of gasses into and out of the leaf.

b) Fix CO_2 into carbohydrate.

c) Absorb light energy and transfer it to an electron.

d) Both B and C are correct

16. The vascular tissue in a root conducts water and food. Where does the food come from?

a) It is made in the leaves and stem and transported to the root

b) The root absorbs the food from the soil.

c) The food is absorbed from the air by the leaves and transported to the root

d) It is made in the root.

17. Which cell type is best for conducting water?

a) Sieve tube element b) Collenchyma

c) Tracheid d) Parrenchyma

18. What role does cohesion force play in the process of water movement from roots to leaves?
    a) It causes the water molecules to adhere to the cell walls of the xylem cells
    b) It causes an acceleration in photosynthesis
    c) It causes the column of water to act as a continuous chain
    d) It causes evaporation to occur in all directions
19. The cohesion-tension theory of water movement in the xylem states that when water evaporates from the plant through the stomata, it pulls additional water from the xylem due to water's cohesive nature. The resulting tension in the xylem-
    a) Pulls more water up from the roots.
    b) Causes the xylem cells to collapse
    c) Pulls more water from the surrounding leaf tissue
    d) Causes the stem to expand.
20. Why it is possible for the Calvin cycle to occur in the dark?
    a) It is not possible for any part of photosynthesis to occur without light.
    b) None of the products of the light-dependent reactions are involved in the Calvin cycle.
    c) The Calvin cycle obtains energy from sugars made previously by the light-dependent reactions of photosynthesis.
    d) The Calvin cycle uses energy stored previously during the light-dependent reactions of photosynthesis.
21. Which of the following is true for respiration?
    a) Light respiration occur in leaves while dark respiration occur in all living plant tissues
    b) Both light and dark respiration occur in all living tissues.
    c) Light respiration occur in aerial parts of the plant while dark respiration occur in roots.
    d) None of the above

22. Soil respiration also affects productivity of forest. The soil respiration is more in broadleaf forest then conifers. The increased soil respiration in broadleaf forest is due to

    a) Soil remains moist under broadleaf forest because they transpire less then conifers.

    b) It may be due to presence of more soil microbes under broadleaf forest.

    c) Broadleaf decompose earlier and provide less insulation on the soil surface.

    d) All of these

23. Net Primary Productivity of forest depends on

    a) Energy capturing surface

    b) Water and nutrient availability

    c) Length of growing season

    d) All of these

24. During reforestation, net productivity is

    a) At early stage it is large, then at maturity it will reaches up to zero

    b) At early stage it is lowest and gradually at maturity it will reaches highest.

    c) It remains constant over time.

    d) None of these

25. ———— contribute maximum portion of sun light reaching on earth.

    a) UV light b) Visible light

    c) Infra red light d) All have equal proportion

26. Maximum portion of infrared is filleted by atmosphere because of

    a) Ozone layer b) Water vapour

    c) CO_2 and Ozone d) None of these

27. In rainforest, under storey plants have
    a) Less induction period for photosynthesis
    b) Higher induction period for photosynthesis
    c) Similar induction period as required by upper storey tree for photosynthesis
    d) None of these
28. Canopy density indicate
    a) Number of leaves per unit canopy volume
    b) Leaf weight per unit canopy volume
    c) Leaf area per unit canopy volume
    d) All of the above
29. Which of the following is true for shade plants?
    a) They can absorb more light and their photosynthesis is saturated at low light
    b) They can absorb less light and thus their photosynthesis is saturated at low light
    c) They can absorb similar light as a sun plant but their photosynthesis is saturated at low light
    d) None of the above
30. Xanthophyll cycle protects photosynthesis machinery from excess light. In the cycle excess energy is used for:
    a) Conversion of violaxanthin to zeaxanthin
    b) Conversion of zeaxanthin to violaxanthin
    c) A and B both
    d) None of these
31. Shade adopted plants have low light compensation points, it means
    a) They require high light intensity to fix CO_2 as compared to sun plants.
    b) They achieve net gain in CO_2 at lower light levels as compared to sun adopted plants.
    c) They have higher rate of respiration at lower light intensity.
    d) All of the above

32. Heartwood is
    a) Physiologically active xylem tissues
    b) Physiologically active phloem tissues
    c) Physiologically inactive xylem tissues
    d) Physiologically in active phloem tissues
33. As light intensity increases up to 50% of full sunlight, photosynthesis of C3 plants
    a) Become light saturated earlier than C4 plants
    b) Is not light saturated, C4 plants photosynthesis is light saturated
    c) Both can behave similarly
    d) None of these
34. Gas exchange is NOT a limiting factor for photosynthesis in
    a) Dense stand of agronomic crops
    b) Dense stand of young trees
    c) Stands of Mature trees
    d) None of the above
35. As air temperature warms during the day, the rate of photosynthesis tends to increase. Why?
    a) Warm O_2 is more reactive than cool O_2.
    b) Warm CO_2 is less reactive than cool CO_2
    c) Stomata close to conserve water and CO_2
    d) Enzyme rates increase with moderate warming.
36. Vascular plant tissue includes all of the following cell types EXCEPT
    a) Vessels b) Companion cells
    c) Sieve cells d) Cambium cells
37. Which functional plant cells lack a nucleus?
    a) Xylem only
    b) Sieve tube cells only
    c) Companion cells only
    d) Both xylem and sieve tube cells
    e) Both companion and parenchyma cells

38. All of the following cell types are correctly matched with their functions EXCEPT
   a) Mesophyll/photosynthesis.
   b) Sieve tube member/translocation of sugars.
   c) Vessel element/water transport.
   d) Companion cell/formation of secondary xylem and phloem.

39. According to the pressure-flow hypothesis of phloem transport,
   a) Solute moves from a high concentration in the "source" to a lower concentration in the "sink."
   b) Water is actively transported into the "source" region of the phloem to create the turgor pressure needed.
   c) The combination of a high turgor pressure in the "source" and transpiration water loss from the "sink" moves solutes through phloem conduits.
   d) The pressure in the phloem of a root is normally greater than the pressure in the phloem of a leaf.

40. Transport of water through the xylem is
   a) Passive, requiring no energy expenditure by the plant.
   b) Passive, unless the soil is very dry.
   c) Active, requiring energy expenditure by the plant.
   d) Active, requiring energy expenditure by the soil.

41. Seeds of plant species native to habitats where wildfires are frequent must be exposed to smoke or fire before they will germinate because
   a) Fire kills animals that would eat the seeds before germination.
   b) Smoke provides vital nutrients.
   c) Smoke shields the seeds from harmful solar radiation.
   d) Fire clears away other plants that might compete for sunlight and nutrients.

42. When guard cells sense blue or red light, they swell open to allow gas exchange. Why do they respond only to these wavelengths of light?

    a) Sunlight is made up of a combination of only these wavelengths.

    b) These wavelengths are found only in early morning light.

    c) These are the wavelengths of light used in photosynthesis.

    d) These wavelengths are found only in late evening light.

43. A concentration gradient of water vapour between the atmospheric air and intercellular spaces of leaves is created by

    a) The accumulation of water vapour in the intercellular spaces of mesophyll which was created by the sunlight on the surface of mesophyll cell walls.

    b) The water in the cells filling the intercellular spaces of leaves

    c) The translocated water with the mesophyll cells of leaves through Xylem tissue

    d) The water present in the large intercellular spaces and large number of stomata on the leaves

44. The main function of mycorrhiza is

    a) Absorption of water   b) Absorption of phosphates

    c) Protection from bacteria   d) Defense from insects

45. What is a property of C4 plants, but not C3 plants?

    a) Initially fix carbon dioxide in mesophyll cells as 4-carbon long compounds.

    b) Initially fix carbon dioxide in bundle sheath cells as 3-carbon long compounds.

    c) Initially fix carbon dioxide in mesophyll cells as 3-carbon long compounds.

    d) Initially fix carbon dioxide in budle sheath cells as 4-carbon long compounds

46. Senescence in deciduous trees is
    a) Whole plant senescence b) Sequential senescence
    c) Synchronous senescence d) Shoot senescence
47. An example of paradormancy is:
    a) Dormancy due to presence of inhibitor
    b) Dormancy due to immature embryo
    c) Lateral bud dormancy due to apical bud
    d) All of the above
48. All of the following are true of tracheids EXCEPT
    a) They are packed together to form vascular tissue.
    b) They contain cytoplasm.
    c) They are found in all modern phyla of vascular plants.
    d) They die after maturing.
49. Seed dormancy is not a common phenomenon in trees of
    a) Northern hemisphere b) Arid and semi arid tropics
    c) Moist tropics d) Southern hemisphere
50. Most of conifer show :
    a) Epigeal germination b) Hypogeal germination
    c) Intermideate type d) All of these
51. Seeds when soaked in water imbibe because
    a) Osmotic pressure inside the seed is low
    b) Seed coat contain lot of salts
    c) The process of absorption work
    d) There are many vacuoles in the endosperm
52. Supra optimal concentration of auxin:
    a) Promote flowering
    b) Kills the plant
    c) Prevent shortening of the internodes
    d) Promote growth in both stem and root apex

53. Respiration is:
    a) Exothermic process b) Endothermic process
    c) Endergonic process d) Anabolic process

54. Tree species growing in semi arid and arid area of tropics, have seed dormancy due to:
    a) Immature embryo b) Presence of inhibitors
    c) Seed coat d) No seed dormancy

55. The light utilization coefficient (γ) for Forest is :
    a) Greater than crop land b) Less than crop land
    c) Equal to crop land d) None of these

56. Higher form quotient indicate :
    a) Greater stem volume b) Lower stem volume
    c) Greater wood density d) Lower wood density

57. You will find more circular stem in :
    a) Angiosperm trees b) Gymnosperm trees
    c) Mangroves d) Orchids

58. All underground plant part are coated with :
    a) Suberin b) Cutin
    c) Wax d) All of these

59. High chlorophyll to Rubisco ratio is observed in:
    a) Sun plants b) Shade plants
    c) Both have same ratio d) None of these

60. Small chloroplast, small thick leaves and low leaf area ratio are characteristic features of :
    a) Sun plants b) Shade plants
    c) Tundra vegetation d) Tropical vegetation

61. Shade plant chloroplast have:
    a) More appressed region in thylakoid membrane with more PS II molecules
    b) Less appresed region in thylakoid membrane with more PS II molecules

c) Less appresed region in thylakoid membrane with less PS II molecules

d) More appresed region in thylakoid membrane with less PS II molecules

62. Photosynthetic quantum yield is

a) Less in shade plant while higher in sun plant

b) Higher in shade plant while lower in sun plant

c) Same in sun and shade plants

d) None of these

63. Sun plants have higher light compensation point as compared to shade plants it is due to differences in respiration rate. Respiration rate may differ in these plants because :

a) Increased carbohydrate processing in sun plants and (3).

b) Increased costs of constructing sun leaves

c) A higher cost of maintaining sun leaves

d) All of these

64. Above P_{max}, at given photon irradiance level:

a) Sun plant experience more excess light as compared to shade plants.

b) Shade plant experience more excess light as compared to sun plants.

c) Both plants experience more excess light.

d) None of these

65. Light interception by canopy understand by Beer Lambert law $\{I = I_0 \exp(-kL)\}$, in which k is an extinction coefficient. Higher value of k of a canopy indicate:

a) Photon irradiance not decrease with canopy depth

b) Photon irradiance decrease with canopy depth

c) Photon irradiance increases with canopy depth

d) None of these

Answer Key of Paper-V

1.	**b**	2.	**b**	3.	**a**	4.	**c**	5.	**d**	6.	**c**	7.	**a**	8.	**a**
9.	**a**	10.	**d**	11.	**b**	12.	**d**	13.	**b**	14.	1(**d**)	2(**d**)		15.	**a**
16.	**a**	17.	**c**	18.	**a**	19.	**a**	20.	**d**	21.	**a**	22.	**d**	23.	**d**
24.	**a**	25.	**b**	26.	**b**	27.	**a**	28.	**c**	29.	**c**	30.	**a**	31.	**b**
32.	**c**	33.	**a**	34.	**c**	35.	**d**	36.	**d**	37.	**d**	38.	**d**	39.	**a**
40.	**a**	41.	**d**	42.	**b**	43.	**c**	44.	**b**	45.	**a**	46.	**c**	47.	**c**
48.	**b**	49.	**c**	50.	**a**	51.	**c**	52.	**b**	53.	**a**	54.	**c**	55.	**b**
56.	**a**	57.	**b**	58.	**a**	59.	**b**	60.	**a**	61.	**a**	62.	**c**	63.	**d**
64.	**b**	65.	**b**												

6

Plant Breeding

1. A single seed is saved from each surviving plant to generate next generation in
   a) Backcross method b) Bulk method
   c) SSD method d) Pedigree method
2. Heterosis over commercial hybrid is known as
   a) Standard heterosis b) Heterobeltiosis
   c) Average Heterosis d) Hybrid vigour
3. A progeny of single self fertilized homozygous individual is
   a) Clone b) Pureline
   c) Multiline d) Hybrid
4. Random mating population is also known as
   a) Panmictic population b) Mendelian population
   c) Mass population d) Both A & B
5. The MS system in which, male sterile and fertile plants produced in 1 : 1 proportion is
   a) GMS b) CGMS
   c) CMS d) Biparental mating
6. The bulk method of breeding first used by
   a) Nilsson and Ehle b) Johnson
   c) Peterson d) Stadler
7. Protogyny condition is observed in
   a) Maize b) Sugarbeet
   c) Bajra d) Okra

8. The potent mutagen which is used to induce male sterility in cytoplasmic gene or plasma gene is

a) GA_3 b) Ethidium Bromide

c) $AgNO_3$ d) CCC

9. The source of MS gene in pearlmillet is

a) Dee-gee-woo-gen b) Kafir 60

c) Tift 23A d) Norin 10

10. The chief objective of long term bulking is

a) To allow natural selection b) For increasing yield

c) To allow artificial selection d) None of the above

11. The process of bringing wild species under human management is referred as

a) Acclimatization b) Conservation

c) Introduction d) Domestication

12. The first artificial plant hybrid was produced by

a) Koelreuter b) Mendel G.

c) Nilsson and Ehle d) Thomas fairchild

13. The random change in gene frequency due to sampling error is

a) Genetic load b) Genetic drift

c) Genetic erosion d) Gene shift

14. The prerequisite for crop improvement is

a) Genetic variation b) Sexual reproduction

c) Pollination control d) Cytoplasmic male sterility

15. Genetic make-up of the clone is

a) Homogeneous b) Heterozygous

c) Homozygous d) None of these

16. The father of green revolution in the world is

a) B. P. Pal b) A. Howard

c) M. S. Swaminathan d) N. E. Borlaug

17. The term nobilization is related to
   a) Wheat b) Rice
   c) Sugarcane d) Soyabean
18. The world's first cotton hybrid was developed in 1970 by
   a) M. L. Singh b) C. T. Patel
   c) P. Maheshwari d) K. N. Kadapa
19. The toxic substance present in *brassica oil* is
   a) Erucic acid b) HCN
   c) BOAA d) Dhurin
20. The source of dwarfing gene is rice
   a) Norin 10 b) Cry 1 AC
   c) Bt-101 d) Dee-geo-woo-gen
21. The source of dwarfing gene is wheat
   a) Norin 10 b) Cry 1 AC
   c) Bt-101 d) Dee-geo-woo-gen
22. The characteristics of tropical canes is
   a) Thick stem & high sugar content
   b) Thin stem & high sugar content
   c) Thick stem & low sugar content
   d) Thin stem & low sugar content
23. The world's first hybrid of cotton developed by Dr. C.T. Patel was
   a) H 6 b) H 4
   c) H 2 d) Varalaxmi
24. The world's first inter-specific hybrid in cotton is
   a) Varalaxmi b) Jayalaxmi
   c) Laxmi d) CBS 156
25. The world's first cotton hybrid (H-4) is the cross between
   a) *G. hirsutum x G. hirsutum*
   b) *G. barbadense x G. Hirsutum*

c) *G. hirsutum* x *G. barbadense*

d) *G. hirsutum* x *G. Raimondii*

26. The male parent of world's first cotton hybrid (H 4) is

a) G Cot 67 b) Laxmi

c) American necteriless d) Varalaxmi

27. The female parent of world's first cotton hybrid (H 4) is

a) G Cot 67 b) G Cot 57

c) G cot 87 d) Varalaxmi

28. The texas cytoplasm (CMS-T) of maize is vulnerable to

a) Ergot b) Helminthosporium blight

c) Late blight d) Downey mildew

29. The Tift 23A cytoplasm of bajra is vulnerable to

a) Powdery mildew b) Helminthosporium blight

c) Late blight d) Downey mildew

30. The concept of center of origin was given by

a) Thomas fairchild b) Hugo de Vris

c) N. I. Vavilov d) N. P. Robinson

31. The example of primary introduction in wheat is

a) Lok-1 b) Lerma Rojo

c) Sonalika d) Kalyan Sona

32. The NBPGR center representing tropical zone is

a) Simla b) Kanya Kumari

c) Jodhpur d) Amravati

33. Forest Research Institute is located at

a) Jobner b) Wellington

c) Dehradun d) Culcutta

34. The example of secondary introduction in wheat is

a) Sonora 64 b) Lerma Rojo

c) Kalyan sona d) Lok-1

35. In India, the implementation of DIP act started from
    a) 1912 b) 1913
    c) 1914 d) 1915
36. The process of adaptation of a variety to a new environment is
    a) Evaluation b) Acclimatisation
    c) Conservation d) Multiplication
37. The extent of acclimatisation is determined by
    a) Mode of pollination
    b) Amount of genetic variability
    c) Duration of crop cycle
    d) All of these
38. The considerable reservoir of the variability is
    a) Land races b) Composite variety
    c) Open pollinated varieties d) All of these
39. Gradual loss of variability from cultivated and wild background is referred as
    a) Genetic imbalance b) Genetic homeostasis
    c) Genetic erosion d) None of these
40. Trips for the purpose of collection of various forms of crop plants and related species is
    a) Exploration b) Expansion
    c) Conservation d) Multiplication
41. In India, the flag smut of wheat disease was introduced from
    a) Austria b) Ceylon
    c) Australia d) Pakistan
42. A vegetative reproduction –bulbil is observed in
    a) Mint b) Garlic
    c) Bunda d) Ginger
43. The situation in which synergids and antipodal cells are developed into an embryo is
    a) Apogamy b) Parthenogenesis
    c) Apospory d) Diplospory

44. Cleistogamy condition is observed in
    a) Tomato b) Bajra
    c) Brinjal d) Oat
45. The cleistogamy condition promotes
    a) Self pollination b) Often cross pollination
    c) Cross pollination d) None of the above
46. The often cross pollinated crop is
    a) Alfalfa b) Linseed
    c) Cucumber d) Sorghum
47. The Dioecy condition is observed in
    a) Papaya b) Date palm
    c) Spinach d) All of these
48. The crop in which pistil mature before stamen is
    a) Bajra b) Rice
    c) Sorghum d) Maize
49. Protandry condition is observed in:
    a) Bajra b) Alfalfa
    c) Sugarbeet d) None of these
50. Loss of vigour due to inbreeding is common in
    a) Self pollinated crop
    b) Cross pollinated crop
    c) Vegetatively propagated crop
    d) Both b & c
51. The classification of self incompatibility was given by
    a) East and Mangelsdorf b) Lewis
    c) Hughes and Babcock d) Edwardson
52. The self incompatibility reaction of pollen is depends upon its own genotype in
    a) Sporophytic system b) Heteromorphic system
    c) Gametophytic system d) Both A & B

53. The self incompatibility is associated with morphological differences of flower is:

a) Sporophytic system b) Heteromorphic system

c) Gametophytic system d) Both A & C

54. The major drawback of GMS system for hybrid seed production is

a) Roguing of male fertile plant

b) Maintenance of fertile plant

c) Maintenance of sterile plant

d) F_1 become sterile

55. The GMS system is used for hybrid seed production in

a) Tomato b) Cotton

c) Okra d) All of these

56. The CMS system is used in

a) Tomato b) Cotton

c) Tobacco d) Sorghum

57. The major drawback of CGMS system is

a) Unsatisfactory pollination

b) Unsatisfactory fertility restoration

c) Breakdown of male sterility

d) All of these

58. Conservation of germplasm under natural condition is called as

a) *In situ* conservation b) Gene bank

c) *Ex situ* conservation d) Obsolate cultivar

59. Seed which dried at low moisture content and stored at low temperature without losing their viability are

a) Recalcitrant seeds b) Active seeds

c) Orthodox seeds d) Certified seeds

60. The character whose development is depend upon specific environment is

a) Quantitative chracter b) Threshold character

c) Qualitative character d) None of these

61. Gene pool consists of
   a) Modern cultivars
   b) Advanced breeding materials
   c) Land races
   d) All the above
62. The variety of genotypes found in a particular crop species are
   a) Genetic diversity b) Genetic erosion
   c) Gene sanctuaries d) Field gene banks
63. Germplasm collected within the country is known as
   a) Active collection b) Working collection
   c) Indigenous collection d) Exotic collection
64. Primitive cultivars which are selected and cultivated by farmers for many years are
   a) Extent variety b) Obsolete cultivar
   c) Land races d) Modern cultivar
65. A place, region or area where maximum variability of crop plants observed is known as
   a) Genetic diversity b) Micro-centers
   c) Gene sanctuaries d) Centre of diversity
66. Protogyny condition is observed in
   a) Pearlmillet b) Sorghum
   c) Maize d) Sugarbeet
67. A type of cell division which generate variability is
   a) Mitosis b) Meiosis
   c) Amitosis d) Fission
68. Artificial vegetative reproduction is done by
   a) Grafting b) Budding
   c) Layering d) All the above
69. Development of embryo from egg cell without fertilization is known as
   a) Apogamy b) Parthenogenesis
   c) Apospory d) Autogamy

70. Self pollination is associated with

a) Herkogamy b) Dichogamy

c) Dicliny d) Homogamy

71. Mating system in which each female gamete has equal chance to unite with every male gamete is known as:

a) Genetic assortative mating

b) Genetic disassortative mating

c) Random mating

d) None of the above

72. Genetic variances partitioned into additive and non additive component by

a) R. A. Fisher (1918) b) Sewall Wright (1935)

c) Mather and Jinks (1982) d) D. S. Falconer (1960)

73. Additive genes exhibit

a) Complete dominance b) Incomplete dominance

c) Lack of dominance d) Overdomiance

74. Additive genetic variances is related with

a) Homozygosity b) Narrow sense heritability

c) Transgressive segregation d) All of these

75. Dominance variance has relationship with

a) Heterozygosity b) Heterosis

c) Specific Combining Ability d) All of these

76. Dominance variance results due to

a) Intra-allelic interaction b) Inter-allelic interaction

c) Cytoplasmic effect d) All of these

77. The real epistatic is:

a) Additive x Additive b) Additive x Dominance

c) Dominance x Dominance d) None of these

78. A MS system which is controlled by both cytoplasmic and nuclear genes is

a) GMS b) CMS

c) CGMS d) All the above

79. The intensity of inbreeding is measured by

a) CV

b) Calculated F

c) CD

d) Coefficient of inbreeding (F)

80. Pureline theory was developed by

a) Thoday (1960) b) Mather (1951)

c) Allard (1960) d) Johannsen (1903)

81. The concept of multiline varieties was developed by

a) Falconer (1960) b) Goulden (1939)

c) Jensen (1952) d) Johannsen (1903)

82. A heterogeneous population includes

a) Composite variety b) Multiline variety

c) Synthetic variety d) All the above

83. Homozygous populations include

a) Inbred lines b) Multilines

c) Pure lines d) All the above

84. A single seed descent method is first used by Grafius (1965) in

a) Wheat b) Barley

c) Oat d) Rice

85. The most effective method for the transfer of oligogenic characters is

a) Bulk method b) Back cross method

c) Pedigree method d) Disreptive method

86. Difference between mean phenotypic value of the progeny of selected plants and the parental population is known as

a) Genetic gain
b) Genetic advance
c) Heritability
d) Coheritability

87. Ratio of additive variance to phenotypic variance is called

a) Heritability (Broad sense)
b) Heritability (Narrow sense)
c) Coheritability
d) Genetic gain

88. Somatic hybridization is useful in

a) Producing allo-tetraploid in one step
b) Bypassing sexual process
c) Conserving heterosis
d) All of these

89. In half diallel, total crosses among parents are equal to

a) P(P-1)/2
b) P(P-1)
c) P(P+1)/2
d) P(P+1)

90. In full diallel, total number of crosses among P parents would be

a) P (P-1)/2
b) P (P+1)/2
c) P (P-1)
d) P^2

91. *Erucic acid* is found in

a) Soybean
b) Safflower
c) Mustard
d) Lathyrus

92. Neurotoxin is found in

a) Chickpea
b) Okra
c) Sorghum
d) Pearl millet

93. In random mating population, coefficient of inbreeding is

a) 0
b) 1/2
c) 1
d) 2

94. A process which leads to transfer of some genes from one species to another is known as

a) Interspecific hybridization b) Intervarietal hybridization

c) Intergeneric hybridization d) Intra-specific hybridization

95. General combining ability is estimated from

a) Half sib crosses b) Full sib crosses

c) a & b above d) None of these

96. Specific combining ability is estimated from

a) Half sib crosses b) Full sib crosses

c) a & b above d) None of these

97. The concept of plant ideotype was developed by

a) Donald (1968) b) Adams (1982)

c) Jennings (1964) d) None of these

98. First intergeneric hybrid between raddish and cabbage was made by

a) Andrew Knight (1800) b) Rimpu (1890)

c) Karpechenko (1927) d) Hull (1945)

99. National Research Center for onion and garlic is located at

a) Pune b) Nanded

c) Nashik d) Aurangabad

100. In gametophytic system of self incompatibility, partial fertility will be result from

a) S_1S_2 x S_1S_2 b) S_1S_2 x S_1S_3

c) S_1S_2 x S_3S_4 d) None of these

101. Self incompatibility reaction may occur

a) On the stigma b) In the style

c) In the ovary d) All of these

102. Homogeneous-homozygous population includes

a) Pure lines b) Inbred lines

c) Both a & b d) None of these

103 Heterogeneous-heterozygous population includes

a) Synthetic variety b) Composite variety

c) Segregating generation d) All of these

104. Concept of single seed descent method was developed by

a) Goulden (1939) b) Shull (1908)

c) Brim (1966) d) Falconer (1960)

105. Wheat varieties KSML 3, MLKS 11 and KML 7404 are

a) Exotic varieties b) Pureline cultivars

c) Multiline varieties d) Mass selection varieties

106. Undesirable linkage can be broken more effectively by

a) Pedigree method b) Backcross method

c) Diallel Selective Mating (DSM) d) Bulk mehod

107. Reciprocal Recurrent Selection is used when a character is govern by

a) Additive genes b) Non additive genes

c) Both a & b d) Cytoplasmic genes

108. Recurrent selection for GCA is effective with

a) Incomplete dominance b) Complete dominance

c) Overdominance d) All of these

109. Disruptive selection is a form of

a) Pureline selection b) Mass selection

c) Recurrent selection d) Clonal selection

110. Overdominance hypothesis is also called as

a) Super dominance b) Single gene heterosis

c) Stimulation of heterozygosity d) All of these

111. Heterosis can be fully exploited in the form of

a) Hybrids b) Composites

c) Synthetics d) Multilines

112. *Brassica juncea* is an amphidiploid between
   a) *B. nigra* and *B. oleracea*
   b) *B. nigra* and *B. campestris*
   c) *B. oleracea* and *B. campestris*
   d) None of these
113. In cotton, jassids have non-preference for
   a) Smoothness of leaves b) Hairiness of leaves
   c) Frago bract d) Okra leaves
114. In maize, resistance to European corn borer is associated with
   a) Waxiness of leaves b) High benzyl alcohol
   c) High DIMBOA in leaves d) High silica content in stem
115. In horizontal resistance, the reproduction rate of pathogen is
   a) $r = 0$ b) $r = 1$
   c) $r > 0$ but < 1 d) Both a & b
116. Concept of gene for gene hypothesis was developed in
   a) Linseed b) Garden pea
   c) Safflower d) Brassica
117. Drought is indicated by
   a) Leaf rolling
   b) Increase in abscisic acid level
   c) Increase in proline level
   d) All of these
118. The order of damage caused by various organism is:
   a) Fungi>Bacteria>Viruses>Nemetode
   b) Fungi>Viruses>Bacteria>Nemetode
   c) Fungi>Nemetode >Viruses> Bacteria
   d) Bacteria> Fungi>Viruses>Nemetode
119. Screening of air borne diseases are possible through
   a) Infector row technique b) Mechanical injury
   c) Sick plot d) None of these

120. In self pollinated crop, coefficient of inbreeding is

a) 0 b) 1

c) 1/2 d) 2

121. The technique utilize for the development of virus free plants is:

a) Micro culture b) Ovule culture

c) Meristem culture d) Protoplast culture

122. An artificially synthesized alloploid - *Raphanobrassica* was made by:

a) Shull b) Karpechenko

c) Mendel d) Devenport

123. The triple fusion leads to development of

a) Embryo b) Zygote

c) Antipodal cells d) Endosperm

124. Which of the following is not a part of the structure of DNA?

a) Phosphate b) Thymine

c) Cytosine d) Ribose sugar

125. The progeny test was developed by

a) Louis de Vilmorin b) Louis Cornvillus

c) Mendel d) Batesman

126. Segregating generations can be handled with

a) Pedigree method b) Backcross method

c) Bulk method d) All of these

127. With every selfing, heterozygosity is reduced by

a) 25 % b) 50 %

c) 75 % d) 100 %

128. In cross pollinated crop, coefficient of inbreeding is

a) 0 b) 1

c) 1/2 d) 2

129. Pureline selection is known as
 a) Mass selection b) Individual plant selection
 c) Modified mass selection d) None of the above
130. The father of green revolution in India is:
 a) B. P. Pal b) N. E. Borlaug
 c) M. S. Swaminathan d) C. T. Patel
131. Concept of combining ability was first proposed by:
 a) Sprague and Tatum (1942) b) Cavali (1952)
 c) Mather (1956) d) Wright (1951)
132. In line X tester cross, each male is crossed with
 a) Different set of females b) Same set of males
 c) Same set of females d) All the above
133. In half diallel, total crosses among parents are equal to:
 a) P(P-1)/2 b) P(P-1)
 c) P(P+1)/2 d) P(P+1)
134. *Pomato* is a combination of
 a) Potato and Tomato b) Potato and Tobacco
 c) Potato and Brinjal d) Sweet potato and Tomato
135. F_1 cross with an OP variety is known as:
 a) Top crosses b) Biparental crosses
 c) Double top cross d) Test cross
136. Ratio of genotypic covariance to phenotypic covariance is called as
 a) Heritability b) Genetic gain
 c) Coheritability d) Genetic advance
137. Selection should be effective in pedigree method from
 a) F_2 onward b) F_4 onward
 c) F_3 onward d) F_6 onward
138. Heterosis can be fixed by
 a) Apomixis b) Polyploidy
 c) Asexual reproduction d) All of the above

139. Monoploids are represented by

a) x | b) 2x
c) n | d) 2n

140. Allopolyploidy is referred to as

a) Hybrid polyploidy | b) Simple polyploidy
c) Segmental polyploidy | d) None of these

141 A nullisomic individual is represented by

a) 2n - 1 | b) 2n + 1
c) 2n - 2 | d) 2n + 2

142. Non-directional force of evolution is refer to

a) Selection | b) Migration
c) Mutation | d) Random genetic drift

143 The Head quarter of UPOV is situated at

a) Rome | b) New York
c) Geneva | d) Tokyo

144. A cross in which order of male & female parent is reversed is called as

a) Reciprocal cross | b) Top cross
c) Back cross | d) Test cross

145. A disease having regular occurrence at a particular area is called as

a) Epidemic | b) Sporadic
c) Endemic | d) None of the above

146. An asexual progeny of a single plant is known as

a) Variety | b) Race
c) Strain | d) Clone

147. A progeny of a single homozygous plant is known as

a) Pureline | b) Race
c) Inbred line | d) Clone

148. Backcross is crossing of F_1 with
    a) Homozygous recessive parent
    b) Recurrent parents
    c) Either of the parents
    d) None of the above
149. The methods which are used for haploid production:
    a) Anther culture b) Ovule culture
    c) Pollen culture d) All of these
150. Herkogamy favours
    a) Selfpollination b) Cross pollination
    c) Both A and B d) None of the above
151. Heterosis can be partially exploited in the form of
    a) Synthetic and Composite variety
    b) Hybrid variety
    c) Pureline variety
    d) Multiline variety
152. Head quarter of NBPGR is located at
    a) Hyderabad b) Bangalore
    c) New Delhi d) Chennai
153. The differential rate of reproduction is known as:
    a) Domestication b) Germplasm collection
    c) Selection d) Hybridization
154. Homozygosity and Homogeneity is maximum in
    a) Pureline b) Inbred line
    c) Land races d) Synthetic variety
155. The crop which do not show inbreeding depression is:
    a) Carrot b) Rice
    c) Sorghum d) Maize

156. Protection period for field crop varieties in plant breeder's right is:
   a) 10 Years b) 15 Years
   c) 7 Years d) 3 Years
157. Mass selection always based on
   a) Genotype b) Phenotype
   c) Progeny test d) Heritability
158. The "father of plant tissue culture" was:
   a) Moore and Skoog b) A. Howard
   c) G. Haberlandt d) N.E. Borlaug
159. The botanical name of tropical canes is
   a) *Saccharum spontaneum* L. b) *saccharum barberi* L.
   c) *Saccharum officinarum* L. d) *Saccharum sinese* L.
160. The dwarf varieties of wheat are
   a) Lodging resistance b) High yielding
   c) Fertilizer responsive d) All of these
161. Self pollinated species are also known as
   a) Allogamous species b) Autogamous species
   c) Inbreeders d) Both B and C
162. The method of breeding not appropriate for cross pollinated crops is
   a) Mass Selection b) Heterosis breeding
   c) Back cross method d) Pure line selection
163. CIP stands for
   a) International Centre for Potato
   b) International Centre for Papaya
   c) International Center for Peanut
   d) Center for Improvement of Potato
164. *Triticale is*
   a) Man made cereal b) Naturally developed cereal
   c) Usually tetraploid species d) Both A & C

165. The crop which show high inbreeding depression is:
    a) Alfalfa b) Rice
    c) Hemp d) Rye
166. The cultivated banana is:
    a) Diploid b) Allotetraploid
    c) Autotriploid d) Allotriploid
167. The quickest method for developing an improved variety is:
    a) Primary introduction b) Mass selection
    c) Secondary introduction d) Domestication
168. An ancient method of crop improvement is:
    a) Selection b) Hybridization
    c) Introduction d) Mutagenesis
169. Potato is a modified stem and is called as:
    a) Sucker b) Tuber
    c) Bulb d) Corm
170. A self pollinated crop showing 5 to 30% cross pollination is considered as:
    a) Self-pollinated crop
    b) Cross pollinated crop
    c) Often-cross pollinated crop
    d) None of these
171. A self pollinated mechanism - Geitonogamy occurs in:
    a) Maize b) Rice
    c) Barley d) Arhar
172. Cleistogamy promotes
    a) Cross-pollination b) Self-pollination
    c) Geitonogamy d) All of these
173. The crops have homozygous balance and are tolerent to inbreeding is:
    a) Self pollinated crops
    b) Often cross pollinated crops

c) Cross pollinated crops

d) None of the above

174. A breeding procedure in which the segregating population of self pollinated species is grown without selections is:

a) Hybridization
b) Bulk method
c) Pedigree method
d) Back cross method

175. Male sterile line is maintained through

a) Crossing with heterozygotes
b) Crossing with male fertile line
c) Both (A) and (B)
d) None of the above

176. Cross pollination is promote by

a) Dicliny
b) Monoecy
c) Dichogamy
d) All of these

177. The incompatible matting is:

a) Pin x Pin
b) Pin x Thrum
c) Thrum x Pin
d) Both B & C

178. Genetic variability can be created through

a) Hybridization
b) Polyploidy breeding
c) Mutation breeding
d) All of the above

179. The breeding method which is used for the development of isogenic line is:

a) Backcross method
b) Pedigree method
c) Bulk method
d) Single seed descent method

180. A restorer gene is present in

a) Nucleus
b) Both A & B
c) Cytoplasm
d) Mitochondria

181. Progeny developed by continues selfing in cross-pollinated crop is

a) Hybrid
b) Pure line
c) Clone
d) Inbred line

182. *Triticale* was developed from cross between

a) Wheat & Oat
b) Maize &Teonsinte
c) Wheat & Barley
d) Wheat & Rye

183. Maximum variability found in

a) F_1 generation
b) F_2 generation
c) F_3 generation
d) F_4 generation

184. The term genotype and phenotype were proposed by

a) Johannsen
b) Batson
c) Mendel
d) Galton

185. Self-pollination increases

a) Homozygosity
b) Heterozygosity
c) Heterogeneity
d) Homogeneity

186. A breeding method which generally used to improve specific character of a well adapted variety is

a) Backcross method
b) Bulk method
c) Pedigree method
d) Hybridization

187. Purelines can be used

a) As varieties
b) As parents in hybridization
c) For studies on mutation
d) All of these

188. Pureline selection can be applied for the improvement of

a) Local varieties
b) Introduced varieties
c) Old pureline varieties
d) All of these

189. The multiple factor hypothesis was given by

a) Nilsson-Ehle
b) Brim
c) Suneson
d) Harlan

190. Bulk method can be used for
    a) Isolation of homozygous line
    b) Mass selection for certain traits
    c) For natural selection
    d) All of these

191. The idea of multiline varieties was first suggested in 1952 by
    a) Borlaug b) Jenson
    c) Briggs d) Knowels

192. Double monosomic is represented by
    a) 2n - 1 – 1 b) 2n + 1 – 1
    c) 2n - 2 d) 2n– 2 +1

193. Diallel Selective Mating Scheme was proposed by
    a) Jensen (1970) b) Brim (1978)
    c) Briggs (1962) d) Harlan (1967)

194. Genetic variation in purelines may arise due to
    a) Out crossing b) Mechanical mixture
    c) Chromosomal aberrations d) All of these

195. Progeny of a Cross between two genetically different homozygote plants is
    a) Variety b) Test cross
    c) Back cross d) Hybrid or F_1

196. In a random mating population, gene and genotype frequencies will be the same generation after generation if there is no
    a) Selection and migration b) Selection and mutation
    c) Selection and random drift d) All of these

197. In general, the frequency of spontaneous mutation is
    a) $\sim 10^{-3}$ b) $\sim 10^{-6}$
    c) $\sim 10^{-8}$ d) $\sim 10^{-10}$

198. The breeding method which provides information about the mode of inheritance of various qualitative characters which is not possible by other breeding methods is
    a) Back cross method b) Hybridization
    c) Pedigree method d) Mutagenesis

199. Population of cross pollinated species are highly
   a) Heterozygous and heterogeneous
   b) Heterozygous and homogeneous
   c) Homozygous and heterogeneous
   d) Homozygous and homogeneous
200. The colchicines can be used for inducing polyploidy was reported by
   a) Morgan (1910)
   b) Johannsen (1903)
   c) Blackslee (1937)
   d) Stadler (1927)
201. The efficiency of mass selection primarily depends upon
   a) Gene frequencies
   b) Number of gene controlling the trait
   c) Heritability
   d) All of these
202. Simple recurrent selection is most suited for the character which has
   a) Low heritability
   b) Moderate heritability
   c) High heritability
   d) All of the above
203. Recurrent Selection for GCA is used for
   a) Improving GCA
   b) Improving yielding ability
   c) Improving SCA
   d) Both A & B
204. The method which is not useful method for handling segregating populations
   a) Pedigree breeding
   b) Back cross breeding
   c) Bulk breeding
   d) Heterosis breeding
205. It is assumed that a large part of heterosis is the result of
   a) Additive gene effects
   b) Dominance gene effects
   c) Overdominance gene effects
   d) Epistatic gene effects

206. Reciprocal recurrent selection allows selection for
   a) General combining ability
   b) Specific combining ability
   c) Improved population performance
   d) All of these

207. In 1694, sex in plants was discovered by
   a) Knight b) Goss
   c) Camararious d) Leeuwenhoke

208. Wheat crop is
   a) Self pollinated crop
   b) Often cross pollinated crop
   c) Cross pollinated crop
   d) Often self pollinated crop

209. The first sunflower hybrid developed in India is
   a) MSFH -8 b) KBSH-1
   c) APSH-11 d) BSH-1

210. Parent which is used only once in backcross breeding method is:
   a) Recurrent parent b) Donor parent
   c) Both a and b d) None of the above

211. Intervarietal hybridization is also called
   a) Interspecific hybridization b) Distant hybridization
   c) Intraspecific hybridization d) Intergeneric hybridization

212. In the species with small flowers, hand emasculation is generally
   a) Difficult b) Laborious
   c) Time consuming d) All of these

213. Generally, emasculation is done one day before anthesis between
   a) 2.00 – 4.00 PM b) 6.00 – 8.00 AM
   c) 4.00 – 6.00 PM d) 6.00 - 8.00 PM

214. An intergeneric hybrid, *Raphanobrassica* was produced by

a) Karpechenko b) Darwin

c) Rimpau d) Ladzinski

215. Heterobeltiosis is estimated over the

a) Better parent b) Mid parent

c) Standard variety d) Popular variety

216. Selection was possible in F_1 generation in

a) Maize b) Sugarcane

c) Cotton d) Rice

217. The parents used frequently in back cross breeding programme is

a) Non recurrent parent b) Donor parent

c) Recurrent parent d) All of these

218. The most commonly used agent for chromosome doubling is

a) Decapitation b) Callus culture

c) Colchicine d) All of the above

219. The most critical factor in a hybridization programme is

a) Choice of parents

b) Emasculation

c) Handling of segregating generation

d) Pollination

220. The chief purpose of emasculation is

a) To prevent selfing b) To promote crossing

c) To promote seed set d) All of the above

221. Brinjal crop is

a) Self pollinated crop

b) Often cross pollinated crop

c) Cross pollinated crop

d) Often self pollinated crop

222. Which of the following is the most critical during emasculation?
   a) Anthers must not be burst
   b) All the anthers must be removed
   c) Gynoecium must not be damaged
   d) All of these

223. A plant bearing both male and female flowers is said to be
   a) Dioecious b) Monoecious
   c) Polygamous d) Digamous

224. The crops which shows severe inbreeding depression is:
   a) Vegetatively propagated crops
   b) Cross-pollinated crops
   c) Self-pollinated crops
   d) Both A & B

225. Asexually propagated crops are:
   a) Mostly perennial b) Highly heterozygous
   c) Generally polyploidy d) All of these

226. Clones usually degenerate due to:
   a) Viral infection b) Bacterial infection
   c) Mutation d) All of these

227. The newer methods for crop improvement is:
   a) Mutagenesis b) Selection
   c) Hybridization d) Introduction

228. Genetic variation within clones may arise due to
   a) Segregation & recombination
   b) Mechanical mixture
   c) Somatic mutation
   d) All of these

229. A process of formation of pollen grain is known as
   a) Mega-sporogenesis b) Micro-sporogenesis
   c) Mega-gametogenesis d) Micro-gametogenesis

230. The term heterosis was first used in 1914 by

a) East
b) Powers
c) Shull
d) Davenport

231. If there are 60 AA, 36 Aa, and 4 aa individuals in population, the frequencies of A (=p) and a (=q) will be which of the following?

a) p = 0.6, q = 0.4
b) p = 0.66, q = 0.34
c) p = 0.8, q = 0.2
d) p = 0.78, q = 0.22

232. Composite varieties are developed in:

a) Self pollinated crops
b) Clone
c) Cross pollinated crops
d) All of these

233. In a random mating population, the frequency of aa is equal to 0.04, what will be the frequency of a?

a) 0.02
b) 0.20
c) 0.4
d) 0.04

234. The heterosis which has commercial or practical value is:

a) Average heterosis
b) Heterobeltiosis
c) Economic heterosis
d) Luxuriance

235. The dominance hypothesis was first proposed in 1908 by:

a) Beal
b) East
c) Koelreuter
d) Davenport

236. An inbred is crossed with an open-pollinated variety is known as:

a) Top cross
b) Test cross
c) Double top cross
d) Three-way cross

237. General combining ability can be estimated from the performance of

a) Parents
b) Backcrosses
c) F_1 s
d) F_2 s

238. A mutation which kills all the individuals that carry the mutation is known as

a) Lethal mutation b) Sub lethal mutation

c) Vital mutation d) Sub-vital mutation

239. The concept of double cross hybrid was proposed in 1918 by

a) Hays b) Jones

c) Jenkins d) Shull

240. Broader genetic base is found in

a) Mass selection b) Clonal selection

c) Pureline selection d) All of these

241. A mutation which kills more than 50% of the individuals that carry the mutation is known as

a) Lethal mutation b) Sub lethal mutation

c) Vital mutation d) Sub-vital mutation

242. The ultimate source population used for the isolation of inbred lines is

a) Open-pollinated varieties b) Synthetics

c) Single cross hybrids d) Double cross hybrids

243. Yield prediction and reconstitution is possible in case of

a) F_2 generation b) Synthetic variety

c) Composite variety d) OP variety

244. The cross of F_1 with its recessive parent is known as

a) Top cross b) Diallel cross

c) Test cross d) Back cross

245. A transgene, which behaves in transgenic plant as

a) Recessive b) Dominant

c) Co-dominant d) Over dominant

246. The molecular marker which show co-dominant inheritance is:

a) RFLPs b) STMSs

c) Both A & B d) RAPDs

247. Pollination and fertilization occurs before opening of flower is termed as:

a) Chasmogamy b) Homogamy
c) Cliestogamy d) Hetrogamy

248. If 20 inbreds are crossed in all possible combinations, the total number of single crosses (excluding reciprocals) will be

a) 160 b) 175
c) 190 d) 380

249. In male sterile plants, haploid production is possible through

a) Overy b) Stigma
c) Anther d) Style

250. A quantitative trait shows

a) Continuous variation b) Additive gene action
c) Dominance and epistasis d) All of these

251. Crops are classified as cross and self pollinated on the basis of mode of

a) Reproduction b) Pollination
c) Growth d) Development

252. Vertical resistance is also known as

a) Race specific resistance b) Oligogenic resistance
c) Qualitative resistance d) All of the above

253. Concept of gene for gene hypothesis was developed in

a) Linseed b) Oat
c) Gram d) Tomato

254. Under drought condition, there is an increase in

a) Proline level b) Ethylene level
c) Abscisic acid level d) All of the above

255. Drought tolerance is associated with

a) Deep root system
b) Small, waxy and thick leaves

c) Sunken, small and less stomata

d) All of the above

256. Drought is indicated by

a) Increase in proline level b) Increase in ethylene level

c) Leaf rolling d) All of the above

257. Crop ideotype refers to

a) Model plant type b) Good plant model

c) Ideal plant type d) All of the above

258. Concept of ideotype was developed in

a) Oat b) Sorghum

c) Wheat d) Rice

259. The significance difference among several means is tested with the help of

a) F - test b) t - test

c) Z - test d) x^2 test

260. The experimental design which control fertility in two directions are:

a) RBD b) SPD

c) AD d) LSD

261. The experimental design which control fertility in one direction is:

a) RBD b) SPD

c) AD d) LSD

262. Maturation of stamens and pistils at different times in the same flower is called

a) Heterostyle b) Homogamy

c) Dichogamy d) Heterospory

263. Fertilization in a flower occurs in

a) Pollen tube b) Anther

c) Style d) Ovule

264. *Colchicum autumnale* L. belong to the family
 a) Cruciferae b) Liliaceae
 c) Poaceae d) Leguminaseae
265. A bisexual flower which never opens in its life span is called
 a) Cleistogamous b) Dichogamous
 c) Heterogamous d) Homogamous
266. Mixture of isogenic-line is termed as
 a) Synthetic variety b) Purelines
 c) Composite variety d) Multilines
267. A trisomic individual is represented by
 a) 2n-1 b) 2n-2
 c) 2n+1 d) 2n+2
268. Female parent of world first CGMS based Pigeon pea hybrid is
 a) MS(P)DT b) GTR11
 c) GT288A d) GTH-1
269. A soil born disease screening is done in
 a) Infector row b) Mechanical screening
 c) Sick plot d) None of these
270. The mutagen which is base analogue:
 a) EMS b) 5 BU
 c) EES d) MMS
271. CGMS system is used for hybrid seed production in
 a) Chilli b) Bajra
 c) Sorghum d) All of these
272. Multiline variety is deliberate mixture of several
 a) Composite varieties b) Synthetic varieties
 c) Open pollinated varieties d) Isogenic lines
273. Male sterility promotes
 a) Autogamy b) Homogamy
 c) Allogamy d) Dichogamy

274. Homozygous tester is used in
   a) Recurrent selection for GCA
   b) Recurrent selection for SCA
   c) Simple recurrent selection
   d) None of the above

275. The difference between mean phenotypic values of the progeny of selected plants and original population is referred to as
   a) Genetic advance
   b) Selection differential
   c) Genetic gain
   d) None of the above

276. Callus refers to
   a) A group of cells
   b) A mass of unorganized cells
   c) A mass of organized cells
   d) All of the above

277. The process of producing several identical copies of gene sequence is referred to as
   a) Gene cloning
   b) Gene sequencing
   c) Gene splicing
   d) Micro cloning

278. Multiline breeding is exploited widely in
   a) Wheat
   b) Ginger
   c) Cotton
   d) Pigeon pea

279. Hybridization is common in crop like
   a) Wheat
   b) Ginger
   c) Cotton
   d) Rice

280. The one gene one enzyme hypothesis was proposed by
   a) Beadle & Ephrussi
   b) Beadle & Tatum
   c) Brenner
   d) Crick

281. Clonal selection mostly used in the crop
   a) Wheat
   b) Sugarcane
   c) Cotton
   d) Sorghum

282. Progeny of breeder seed is
a) Nucleus seed b) Breeder Seed
c) Foundation seed d) Certified seed

283. The breeding method takes longer period for varietal development is
a) Mass selection b) Bulk method
c) Backcross method d) Pedigree method

284. Inbreeding of cross pollinated species leads to increase in
a) Homozygocity b) Heterozygocity
c) Population mean d) all of the above

285. X^2 test was developed by
a) Fisher b) Karl Pearson
c) Benzer d) Galton

286. Seed act formulated and an acted during
a) 1966 and 1969 b) 1967 and 1968
c) 1967 and 1970 d) 1980 and 1982

287. Analysis of variance permits estimation of
a) Phenotypic variance b) Environmental variance
c) Genotypic variance d) All of these

288. The square root of variance is referred as
a) Standard error b) Coefficient of variation
c) Standard deviation d) Range

289. A healthy plant not setting seed may be due to
a) Self incompatibility b) Male sterility
c) Both a and b d) None of the above

290. Mutation breeding is mostly used in
a) Self pollinated crops
b) Cross pollinated crops
c) Vegetative propagated crops
d) Often cross pollinated crops

291. The ploidy level of commercially cultivated seedless watermelon is

a) Monoploid b) Diploid
c) Triploid d) Tetraploid

292. The standard method of seed moisture estimation is

a) Oven dry method b) Moisture meter
c) Toulene d) P_2O_5 method

293. How many different genotypes are possible when there is a cross of two individuals that are each heterozygous for two genes (a dihybrid cross)?

a) Three b) Nine
c) Seven d) Sixteen

294. If an individual contains two alleles for a particular gene and the two alleles are different from each other, the individual is said to be:

a) Homozygous dominant b) Homozygous recessive
c) Heterozygous d) Hemizygous

295. Heterosis results due to

a) Dominance b) Over dominance
c) Epistasis d) All of the above

296. The Z-test is used when the sample size is

a) 10-20 b) 21-30
c) > 30 d) < 10

297. Metroglyph analysis is based on estimates of

a) Mean b) Covariance
c) Variance d) None of these

298. Seed certification in Gujarat is done by

a) GSSCA b) GSSC
c) GCCS d) GSRC

299. Reciprocal recurrent selection is effective with

a) Incomplete dominance b) Complete dominance
c) Over dominance d) All of the above

300. Which among the following variance is associated with heterosis?

a) GCA
b) SCA
c) Both GCA and SCA
d) None

301. Tag color of Breeder seed certificate is

a) Golden red
b) Golden Yellow
c) Golden Green
d) Ligh Red

302. Hand pollination during commercial seed production is practiced in

a) Sorghum
b) Cotton
c) Pigeonpea
d) Castor

303. A crop showing less than 5% cross pollination is considered as

a) Self pollinated
b) Cross pollinated
c) Often cross pollinated
d) Often self pollinated

304. Quasi diploids are represented by

a) 2n - 1 - 1
b) 2n+1 - 1
c) 2n - 2
d) 2n– 2+1

305. The plant part which can be used for regeneration is called

a) Clone
b) Callus
c) Explant
d) None of these

306. Varietal purity is checked by

a) Grow out test
b) Tz Test
c) Accelerated aging test
d) Germination test

307. Seed testing refers to

a) Purity test
b) Germination test
c) Seed moisture test
d) All of these

308. Seed processing refers to

a) Drying
b) Grading
c) Packing
d) All of these

309. Certified seed tag having

a) Yellow color b) Blue color

c) Red color d) White color

310. The objectives of field inspection is to examine

a) Disease incidence b) Isolation distance

c) Off type plants d) All of these

311. Certification is not required for

a) Breeder seed b) Foundation seed

c) Certified seed d) All of these

312. Scientist has made suggestion to maintain genetic purity of variety was:

a) Mendel b) Horne

c) Shull d) Borlaug

313. Source of breeder seed is

a) Certified seed b) Foundation seed

c) Nucleus seed d) Registered seed

314. During hybridization, information recorded on tags are:

a) Date of emasculation b) Date of pollination

c) Name of the parents d) All of these

315. Certified seed bags are sealed with

a) Golden yellow b) Azure blue

c) White d) Open green

316. Truthful seed bags are sealed with

a) Golden yellow b) Azure blue

c) White d) Opel green

317. Plant of male sterile line growing in male fertile line is known as

a) Off type b) Disease plant

c) Pollen shedder d) Weed plant

318. Synthetic seed is produced by encapsulating somatic embryo with

a) Sodium chloride b) Sodium acetate

c) Sodium alginate d) Sodium nitrate

319. DNA amplification is done in

a) Thermocycler b) Hybridization oven

c) Incubator d) Electrophoresis system

320. An endosperm contain

a) x b) 3n

c) n d) 2n

321. Determining the physical location of a gene or genetic marker on a chromosome is known as

a) Marking b) Mapping

c) Siting d) Taging

322. RAPD are

a) Dominant markers b) Recessive markers

c) Co-dominant marker d) Both A & C

323. During denaturation in PCR, temperature is about

a) 64^0C b) 74^0C

c) 84^0C d) 94^0C

324. Northern blotting techniques used for blotting

a) DNA samples b) Protein samples

c) RNA samples d) All of above

325. PCR system is used for

a) DNA sample quantification b) DNA amplification

c) Visualize DNA samples d) For baking hybridization

326. Southern blotting techniques used for blotting

a) DNA samples b) Protein samples

c) RNA samples d) All of above

327. Thawing is done in warm water at temperature

a) 20-30 ^{0}C
b) -196 ^{0}C
c) 35-45 ^{0}C
d) 10-20 ^{0}C

328. An enzyme that produces internal cuts in nucleic acids is called

a) Endonuclease
b) RNase
c) Exonuclease
d) DNase

329. The major limitation of RAPD is:

a) Cost
b) Reproducibility
c) Tediousness
d) Sequence information

330. The 'natural genetic engineer' is

a) *Agrobacterium*
b) *E.coli*
c) *Azotobacter*
d) *Rhizobium*

331. Specific biomolecules which show easily detectable differences among different strains of a species or among different species is termed as

a) DNA fingerprinting
b) Molecular markers
c) Molecular scissors
d) None of the above

332. Molecular markers include

a) RFLP
b) AFLP
c) RAPD
d) All of the above

333. Molecular markers are used to construct

a) chromosome maps
b) physical maps
c) cytogenetic maps
d) All of the above

334. The variation in the restriction DNA fragment lengths between individuals of a species is called

a) Restriction Fragment Length Polymorphism (RFLP)
b) Random amplified Polymorphic DNA (RAPD)
c) Amplified Fragment Length Polymorphism (AFLP)
d) Simple Sequence repeats (SSR)

335. RFLP is used to
   a) Construct high resolution linkage maps
   b) Identify single gene diseases
   c) Construct QTL maps
   d) All of the above

336. Locations of quantitative genes on chromosomes are called
   a) Qualitative trait loci b) Quatitative trait loci
   c) Both a and b d) None of these

337. The set of DNAs generated by using random primers in a PCR reaction is called
   a) RAPD b) AFLP
   c) RFLP d) SSR

338. The gene for gene hypothesis was given by
   a) Flor b) Priestly
   c) Van der Plank d) Painter

339. The concept of physiological races was first introduced by
   a) Flor b) Knight
   c) Barrus d) Painter

340. Disease escape may be due to
   a) Changed in planting date and site
   b) Early varieties
   c) Pathogen control
   d) All of the above

341. In disease, score 0 indicates
   a) Resistance
   b) Lack of disease symptoms
   c) Lack of pathogen contact
   d) None of the above

342. In Immune reaction, the pathogen reproduction rate is
   a) 0.1 b) 0.25
   c) 0.0 d) 0.75

343. Term Vertical and Horizontal resistance were given by

a) Painter b) Marshal

c) Van der Plank d) Flor

344. The disease resistance mechanisms are

a) Mechanical b) Nutritional

c) Hypersensitivity d) All of the above

345. First study on genetics of disease resistance was reported by

a) Van der Plank b) Biffen

c) Frey d) Barrus

346. The concept of 'Boom and Bust cycle' was given by

a) Flor b) Biffen

c) Frey d) Priestley

347. The gene for gene hypothesis was proposed on the basis of work done on

a) Late blight of potato b) Brown rust on wheat

c) Leaf rust of wheat d) Linseed rust

348. The term 'Vertifolia effect' was given by

a) Frey b) Flor

c) Van der Plank d) Priestley

349. The life cycle of stem rust of wheat was discovered in India by

a) C T Patel b) R P Singh

c) K S Gill d) K C Mehta

350. Southern leaf blight of corn is associated with

a) T-cytoplasm b) C-cytoplasm

c) S-cytoplasm d) None of the above

351. Rust is

a) Air borne disease b) Seed borne disease

c) Soil borne disease d) Insect transmitted disease

352. Epidemic occurrence is common in

a) Seed borne fungi b) Soil borne fungi
c) Air borne fungi d) None of the above

353. The use of multilines to control disease in oats was first suggested by

a) Flor b) Jenson
c) Frey d) Painter

354. The concept of 'clean and dirty crop multiline approach' given by

a) Flor b) Jenson
c) Frey d) Marshall

355. Multiline KSML 3 is based on

a) Sonalika b) Varuna
c) Kalyansona d) Sonora

356. Variety SAR-1(*Striga* Resistant) was developed by

a) NAU, Navsari b) PAU, Ludhiana
c) ICRISAT, Hydrabad d) IARI, New Delhi

357. Insect resistant wheat variety 'Rescue' was first released in

a) Japan (1961) b) Canada (1961)
c) India (1961) d) USA (1961)

358. The abiotic stress includes

a) Salinity b) Acidity
c) alkalinity d) All of the above

359. In disease resistance, monocyclic and polycyclic tests were suggested by

a) Van der plant b) Zodaks
c) Nelson d) Frey

360. Reduction of biomass production per unit due to diseases by

a) Damaging leaf tissues
b) Killing of plants
c) Damaging reproductive organs
d) All of the above

361. A minor disease today may become a major disease tomorrow due to

a) Change in crop varieties

b) Change in agricultural practices

c) Change in pathogen

d) All of the above

362. Disease resistance is a function of

a) Host genotype

b) Host and pathogen genotypes

c) Environment

d) Pathogen genotype

363. New pathotypes arise in fungi due to

a) Recombination

b) Heterokaryosis

c) Mutation and Parasexual reproduction

d) All of the above

364. New races in viruses arise through

a) Recombination b) Both A and C

c) Mutation d) Parasexual reproduction

365. New races in bacteria arise through

a) Recombination b) Mutation

c) Both A and B d) Parasexual reproduction

366. New biotypes are produced in nematodes through

a) Recombination b) Mutation

c) Both A and B d) Parasexual reproduction

367. The disease development stages are greatly affected by environments are

a) Contact b) Infection

c) Both A and B d) Establishment

368. The most important stage for disease escape is
a) Contact b) Infection
c) Establishment d) Reproduction

369. The crucial factor for disease spread is
a) Contact b) Infection
c) Establishment d) Reproduction

370. A variety is called tolerant to a disease if it shows
a) Lower disease score
b) Lower diseases spread
c) Lower reproduction rate
d) Significant lower reduction in yield at same level of diseases attack

371. A cell death in plant is related to
a) Tolerance b) Hypersensitive response
c) Resistance d) Escape

372. Lower reduction in yield compared to susceptible variety is related to
a) Tolerance b) Hypersensitive response
c) Resistance d) Escape

373. Reduced reproduction rate of pathogen in plant is related to
a) Tolerance b) Hypersensitive response
c) Resistance d) Escape

374. Race specific disease resistance is called as
a) Vertical resistance b) Cell death
c) Horizontal resistance d) Hypersensitive reaction

375. Horizontal resistance is governed by
a) Monogenic genes b) Polygenic genes
c) Oligogenic genes d) None of the above

376. Immune response is found in case of
a) Obligate parasites b) Facultative parasites
c) Both A and B d) None of the above

377. Oligogenic disease resistance does not show

a) Pathotype specificity b) Immune reaction

c) Gene for gene relationship d) Continuous variation

378. Biotype differentiation relates primarily to

a) Insects b) Fungi

c) Bacteria d) Viruses

379. Insect resistance may be governed by

a) Oligogenes b) Polygenes

c) Plasmagenes d) All of the above

380. The appearance of new resistance breaking biotypes is affected by

a) Insect species b) Mechanism of resistance

c) Genetics of resistance d) All of the above

381. The plant affected by a disease is known as

a) Host b) Pathogen

c) Both A and B d) Environment

382. The organism that produces the disease is called as

a) Host b) Pathogen

c) Both A and B d) Environment

383. The scientist who noted that cultivated varieties differed in their ability to avoid diseases is

a) Blakeslee b) Fery

c) Theophrastus d) Flor

384. The ability of a pathogen to infect a host strain is called as

a) Tolerance b) Pathogenicity

c) Resistance d) None of the above

385. In fungi, a cell containing two nuclei is called as

a) Monocaryon b) Tricaryon

c) Dicaryon d) None of the above

386. The varieties of a host species used to identify physiological races of a pathogen are known as
 a) Differential hosts b) Host testers
 c) Both A and B d) Ideal differentials

387. Development of any disease depends on a close interaction among
 a) Host b) Pathogen
 c) Environment d) All of the above

388. The different stages of development of fungal diseases are
 a) Contact and infection b) Establishment
 c) Development d) All of the above

389. The process by which the pathogen gains entry into the host tissue is called as
 a) Contact b) Establishment
 c) Development d) Infection

390. The landing of a pathogen on the host tissue is called as
 a) Contact b) Establishment
 c) Development d) Infection

391. Contact and infection stages are greatly affected by
 a) Genotypes b) Variety
 c) Hybrids d) Environment

392. The freedom of susceptible host plants/varieties from a disease purely due to the environmental factors is called as
 a) Disease avoidance or escape
 b) Disease immunity
 c) Disease resistance
 d) Disease tolerance

393. The most prominent factor for disease avoidance or escape is
 a) Avoiding contact
 b) Unfavorable weather conditions
 c) Both A and B
 d) None of the above

394. Disease escape is nuisance because
   a) It reduce yield
   b) It Unable to identify resistant genotype
   c) It reduce quality
   d) All of the above

395. Potassium is known to enhance
   a) Disease resistance
   b) Disease susceptibility
   c) Disease escape
   d) Disease immunity

396. Nitrogen is known to enhance
   a) Disease resistance
   b) Disease susceptibility
   c) Disease escape
   d) Disease immunity

397. To control soil borne fungi and diseases, the highly effective method is
   a) To change the site of planting
   b) To change date of planting
   c) Use balanced NPK
   d) All of the above

398. For controlling the viral diseases, most effective method is
   a) To change the site of planting
   b) To change date of planting
   c) Use balanced NPK
   d) To control the insect vector

399. To protect susceptible varieties, the most effective methods is
   a) To change the site of planting
   b) To change date of planting
   c) Use balanced NPK
   d) Use chemical disease control

400. The range of reactions of host plants to various pathogens may be grouped into
   a) Susceptible b) Resistant and tolerance
   c) Immune d) All of the above

401. The disease development is profuse and is presumably not checked by the genotype of host plant is called as
   a) Susceptible reaction b) Resistant
   c) Immune reaction d) Tolerance

402. When a host plant does not show the symptoms of a disease, it is known as
   a) Susceptible reaction b) Resistant
   c) Immune reaction d) Tolerance

403. Immunity may results due to
   a) Susceptible varieties
   b) Hypersensitive reaction
   c) Prevention of the pathogen in appropriate plant part of host
   d) Both (b) and (c)

404. A group of host cells around the point of infection dies is called as
   a) Susceptible reaction b) Resistant
   c) Hypersensitive reaction d) Tolerance

405. In susceptible reaction, the pathogen reproduction rate is
   a) 1.0 b) 0.25
   c) 0.0 d) 0.75

406. In resistance, the pathogen reproduction rate is
   a) >1.0 b) 0.25
   c) > 0.0 but <1.0 d) < 0.0 but >1.0

407. The less disease development in genotype than that in the susceptible variety is called as
   a) Susceptible reaction b) Resistant
   c) Immune reaction d) Tolerance

408. The given host variety us attacked by the pathogen in the same manner as the susceptible variety, but there is little or no loss in biomass production or yield as known as

a) Susceptible reaction b) Resistant

c) Immune reaction d) Tolerance

409. The name 'Vertifolia effect' derived from the

a) Tomato variety 'Vertifolia'

b) Cucumber variety 'Vertifolia'

c) Potato variety 'Vertifolia'

d) Okra variety 'Vertifolia'

410. An epidemic development in a variety carrying vertical resistance genes and a low level of horizontal resistance, leading to heavy economic losses is known as

a) Vertifolia effect b) Both A and B

c) Boom and Bust cycle d) None of the above

411. The term strong and weak oligogenes given by

a) Frey b) Flor

c) Van der Plank d) Priestley

412. The second gene for gene hypothesis was given by

a) Frey b) Flor

c) Van der Plank d) Priestley

413. A type of resistance where disease progresses at a retarded rate, resulting in intermediate to low disease levels against all pathotypes of a pathogen is called as

a) Slow rusting b) Partial resistance

c) Both (a) and (b) d) Complete resistance

414. A severe outbreak of disease beginning from a low level of infection is known as

a) Disease susceptibility b) Disease endemics

c) Disease epidemics d) All of the above

415. The factors that promotes disease epidemics are

a) Narrow genetic base b) Mono-cropping
c) Introduced pathogen d) All of the above

416. The factors responsible for preventing disease epidemics are

a) Gene pyramiding b) Use multiline varieties
c) Gene deployment d) All of the above

417. A series of resistance genes show some resistance to all the races of pathogens in population is called as

a) Population resistance
b) Synthetic horizontal resistance
c) Both A and B
d) Immune reaction

418. A race of a pathogen which is capable of attacking a host plant with specific resistance is called as

a) Virulent strain b) Avirulent strain
c) Both A and B d) None of the above

419. A race of a pathogen which is unable to attack a host plant having specific resistance is known as

a) Virulent strain b) Avirulent strain
c) Both A and B d) None of the above

420. A strain having a pathogen differing in pathogenicity is known as

a) Host b) Pathogen
c) Parasite d) Physiological race

421. A new strain of an insect in known as

a) Host b) Pathogen
c) Parasite d) Biotype

422. The resistance which gives an effective control of a parasite under field conditions is known as

a) Durable resistance b) Adult resistance
c) Seedling resistance d) Field resistance

423. The long lasting resistance is known as
   a) Durable resistance b) Adult resistance
   c) Seedling resistance d) Field resistance
424. The resistance which is exhibited in early stage of plant growth is known as
   a) Durable resistance b) Adult resistance
   c) Seedling resistance d) Field resistance
425. The resistance which is exhibited in later stage of plant growth is known as
   a) Durable resistance b) Adult resistance
   c) Seedling resistance d) Field resistance
426. In gene for gene hypothesis, the genes in host and pathogen match for all loci, then the host will show
   a) Resistant reaction b) Susceptible reaction
   c) Both A and B d) None of the above
427. A various features of host plant which makes the host undesirable or unattractive to insect for food, shelter or reproduction is known as
   a) Escape or avoidance
   b) Antibiosis
   c) Tolerance
   d) Non preference or non-acceptance
428. The plant characters associated with non-preference are
   a) Colour of leaves b) Leaf angle
   c) Hairiness of stem and leaf d) All of the above
429. An adverse effect of the host on feeding, development and reproduction of insect pest is known as
   a) Escape or avoidance
   b) Antibiosis
   c) Tolerance
   d) Non preference or non-acceptance

430. Antibiosis may involves
   a) Morphological features of host plant
   b) Biochemical features of host plant
   c) Physiological features of host plant
   d) All of the above

431. The mechanisms of insect resistance was given by
   a) Painter b) Marshal
   c) Van der Plank d) Flor

432. The traits like hairiness, colour, thickness and toughness of tissue are called as
   a) Morphological features of host plant
   b) Biochemical features of host plant
   c) Physiological features of host plant
   d) All of the above

433. The traits like osmotic concentration of cell sap and leaf exudates is called as
   a) Morphological features of host plant
   b) Biochemical features of host plant
   c) Physiological features of host plant
   d) All of the above

434. The chemical compounds like high gossypol, tannins, heliocides and silica content are related with
   a) Morphological features of host plant
   b) Biochemical features of host plant
   c) Physiological features of host plant
   d) All of the above

435. The factors affecting durability of insect resistance are
   a) The mode of inheritance of insect resistance
   b) Morphological and biochemical characters associated with insect resistance
   c) Formation of new biotypes
   d) All of the above

436. According to Cramer (1967), the yield losses in plants through insects is

a) 10 % b) 14 %

c) 12 % d) 16 %

437. The annual yield losses through diseases are

a) 10-20 % b) 30-40%

c) 20-30% d) 40-50%

438. The *Orobanche* resistant varieties developed by

a) IARI, New Delhi b) ICARDA, Syria

c) ICRISAT, Hydrabad d) CIMMYT, Maxico

439. The biological methods to control insects are

a) Use of resistant varieties

b) Use of botanical pesticides

c) Use of predators and parasites

d) All of the above

440. The pesticides based on plant extracts is known as

a) Botanical pesticides b) Chemical pesticides

c) Biological pesticides d) All of the above

441. According to painter (1951), the degree of resistance categories are

a) Immunity

b) Susceptible and high susceptible resistance

c) High and low resistance

d) All of the above

442. The mechanisms of insect resistance was given by Painter (1951) are

a) Non preference or non-acceptance

b) Antibiosis

c) Tolerance

d) All of the above

443. The mechanisms of insect resistance was not given by Painter (1951) is
   a) Non preference or non-acceptance
   b) Antibiosis
   c) Tolerance
   d) Escape or avoidance

444. The synonymous of non-preference are
   a) Non-acceptance b) Antixenosis
   c) Both A and B d) Escape

445. A variety of chemicals produced by plants that affect insect behavior is called as
   a) Allelochemicals b) Male gametocytes
   c) Infochemicals d) Chemical pesticides

446. The chemicals which serve as the medium of communication between a plant and an insect species is called as
   a) Allelochemicals b) Male gametocytes
   c) Infochemicals d) Chemical pesticides

447. The major problem of *Striga* weed particularly in the state of
   a) Gujarat b) Uttar pradesh
   c) Rajasthan d) Maharashtra

448. The freedom from insect infestation or damage of an otherwise susceptible host plant purely due to chance is called as
   a) Host b) Tolerance
   c) Host escape d) None of the above

449. The temporary shifts in the environmental conditions that enable a susceptible host to suffer less damage is known as
   a) Ecological resistance b) Apparent resistance
   c) Pseudo-resistance d) All of the above

450. The major pathogens causing disease in living organisms are
   a) Fungi b) Viruses
   c) Bacteria d) All of the above

451. The disease like smut, rust, powdery mildew, Downy mildew were caused by

a) Fungi
b) Viruses
c) Bacteria
d) Nematodes

452. The disease like leaf spots, blights, cankers or wilts are due to

a) Fungi
b) Viruses
c) Bacteria
d) Nematodes

453. The production of microspore and megaspore is known as

a) Megasporogenesis
b) Microsporogenesis
c) Gametogenesis
d) Sporogenesis

454. Seed testing is done for

a) Both genetic and physical purity
b) Germination and vigour of seed
c) Moisture content and seed borne disease
d) All of the above

455. The formula for predicting the F_2 performance of synthetic variety is

a) $F1 - \frac{(F1-P)}{n}$
b) $F1 - \frac{(F1+P)}{n}$
c) $F1 + \frac{(F1-P)}{n}$
d) $F1 + \frac{(F1+P)}{n}$

456. The formula for inbreeding depression is:

a) $\frac{(F1-F2)}{F1} X\ 100$
b) $\frac{(F1+F2)}{F1} X\ 100$
c) $\frac{(F2-F1)}{F1} X\ 100$
d) $\frac{(F2+F1)}{F1} X\ 100$

457. The formula for average heterosis is:

a) $\frac{(F1+MP)}{MP} X\ 100$
b) $\frac{(F1-BP)}{MP} X\ 100$
c) $\frac{(F1-MP)}{MP} X\ 100$
d) $\frac{(F1-MP)}{MP} + 100$

458. The formula for average heterosisbeltiosis is:

a) $\frac{(F1\text{-}BP)}{BP} \times 100$ b) $\frac{(F1\text{-}MP)}{MP} \times 100$

c) $\frac{(F1\text{-}BP)}{BP} \times 100$ d) $\frac{(F1\text{-}CC)}{CC} \times 100$

459. The formula for Economic heterosis is:

a) $\frac{(F1\text{-}CC)}{CC} \times 100$ b) $\frac{(F1\text{-}BP)}{BP} \times 100$

c) $\frac{(F1\text{-}MP)}{MP} X\ 100$ d) $\frac{(F1\text{-}SH)}{SH} \times 100$

460. The formula for standard heterosis is:

a) $\frac{(F1\text{-}CC)}{CC} \times 100$ b) $\frac{(F1\text{-}BP)}{BP} \times 100$

c) $\frac{(F1\text{-}MP)}{MP} X\ 100$ d) $\frac{(F1\text{-}SH)}{SH} \times 100$

461. National Biodiversity Board is located at

a) Calcutta b) Chennai

c) Madras d) New Delhi

462. The observable variation present in a character in a population which includes genotypic and environmental components of variation is known as

a) Phenotypic variation b) Genotypic variation

c) Pathotype variation d) Biotype variation

463. The appearance of a plant with respect to particular character, such as plant height is known as

a) Genotype b) Phenotype

c) Pathotype d) Biotype

464. For hybrids, the seed replacement rate is

a) 50% b) 25%

c) 100% d) 75%

465. The mechanism used for hybrid seed production in Pigeonpea is

a) CMS b) GMS

c) SI d) CGMS

466. The isolation distance for hybrid rice seed production is

a) 50 m b) 100 m

c) 150 m d) 200 m

467. The lines used for production of cucumber are

a) Gynomonoecious b) Monoecious

c) Gynoecious d) Androgynoecious

468. For hybrid seed production, detasseling techniques used in

a) Castor b) Tomato

c) Maize d) Brinjal

469. A chemical act as hybridizing agent is

a) $MnSo_4$ b) GA_3

c) $ZnSo_4$ d) Sodium arsenate

470. For double cross hybrid seed production, the number of inbred lines involved are

a) 2 b) 4

c) 3 d) 6

471. The first Indian vegetable hybrid was released in

a) Ridge gourd b) Bitter gourd

c) Bottle gourd d) Ash gourd

472. Improved seed results in

a) Better germination b) Vigorous seedling growth

c) Higher crop stand d) All of the above

473. Any plant part which is used for commercial multiplication of a crop is called

a) Seed b) Grain

c) Both (a) and (b) d) None of the above

474. The improved seed classes are
   a) Nucleus seed and Breeder seed
   b) Foundation seed
   c) Registered seed and Certified seed
   d) All of the above

475. The production of class of seed which is limited in quantity
   a) Nucleus seed b) Foundation seed
   c) Certified seed d) All of the above

476. The seed produced by originating plant breeder is called as
   a) Nucleus seed b) Breeder seed
   c) Both A and B d) Foundation seed

477. The genetically as well as physically purity of the seed is 100% in
   a) Nucleus seed b) Breeder seed
   c) Both A and B d) None of the above

478. The class of seed which produced under the strict supervision of NSC is
   a) Nucleus seed b) Foundation seed
   c) Certified seed d) Breeder seed

479. The class of seed which produced under the strict supervision of SSCA is
   a) Nucleus seed b) Foundation seed
   c) Certified seed d) Breeder seed

480. The genetically as well as physically purity of the seed is 100% and 98%, respectively in
   a) Foundation seed b) Certified seed
   c) Registered seed d) All of the above

481. Certification is not required in
   a) Nucleus seed b) Breeder seed
   c) Both A and B d) Foundation seed

482. The class of seed in which certification should be done by SSCA

a) Foundation seed b) Certified seed
c) Both A and B d) Breeder seed

483. The basic requirement for seed certifications are

a) Improved variety b) Genetic purity
c) Physical purity d) All of the above

484. In case of certified seed, the contamination by the seeds of another variety is permitted from

a) 0-1% b) 0-0.5%
c) 0-0.2% d) 0-1.5%

485. In case of foundation seed, the contamination by the seeds of another variety is permitted from

a) 0-0.1% b) 0-0.5%
c) 0-0.2% d) 0-1.5%

486. The absence of seeds of other variety of the crop as well as of other crops is known as

a) Germination percentage b) Physical purity
c) Genetic purity d) All of the above

487. The freedom from inert matter and defective seeds is known as

a) Germination percentage b) Physical purity
c) Genetic purity d) All of the above

488. In cucurbits, the minimum germination allowed is

a) 50% b) 60%
c) 55% d) 65%

489. The separation of the field of a variety from that of another variety of the same crop to avoid contamination referred as

a) Rouging b) Physical purity
c) Isolation distance d) Genetic purity

490. The isolation distance of cross pollinated crops are

a) High b) Low
c) Medium d) None of the above

491. The isolation distance of often cross pollinated crops are
   a) High   b) Low
   c) Medium   d) None of the above
492. The isolation distance of self pollinated crops are
   a) High   b) Low
   c) Medium   d) None of the above
493. The isolation distance of cabbage and cauliflower is
   a) 1000 m   b) 1500 m
   c) 1200 m   d) 1600 m
494. The isolation distance of wheat is
   a) 2 m   b) 3 m
   c) 4 m   d) 5 m
495. The process of removal of off type (Phenotypically different) plants from the field of an improved variety is known as
   a) Selfing   b) Roguing
   c) Crossing   d) Hybridization
496. The main objective of rouging is
   a) Prevent selfing
   b) To avoid contamination through mechanical mixture
   c) Better germination
   d) All of the above
497. The rouging should be done at
   a) Before flowering   b) After flowering
   c) Before harvesting   d) All of the above
498. Rouging includes
   a) Off type plants   b) Disease infected plants
   c) Insect infected plants   d) All of the above
499. Breeder seed bags are sealed with
   a) Golden yellow   b) Azure blue
   c) White   d) Open green

500. The lable size of Breeder seed is

a) 15 cm x 10 cm b) 15 cm x 7.5 cm

c) 12 cm x 6 cm d) None of these

501. The lable size of foundation seed is

a) 15 cm x 10 cm b) 15 cm x 7.5 cm

c) 12 cm x 6 cm d) None of these

502. The label size of certified and truthful labeled seed is

a) 15 cm x 10 cm b) 15 cm x 7.5 cm

c) 12 cm x 6 cm d) None of these

503. In gene for gene hypothesis, some gene loci unmatched for host and pathogen, the host will show

a) Resistant reaction b) Susceptible reaction

c) Both A and B d) Immune reaction

504. The adverse conditions caused by such factors for growth and development of crop plants are referred as

a) Abiotic Stress b) Biotic stress

c) Host d) All of the above

505. Abiotic stresses resulting in significant reduction in

a) Yield b) Quality

c) Both A and B d) None of the above

506. In India, the major concern among environmental stresses are

a) Drought b) Salinity

c) Alkalinity d) All of the above

507. The condition of soil moisture deficiency is referred as

a) Drought b) Salinity

c) Alkalinity d) All of the above

508. Soil drought is more common in

a) Arid region b) Semiarid region

c) Steep sloppy region d) All of the above

509. The areas are more prone to drought condition is
    a) Desert area b) Humid area
    c) Both A and B d) Waterlogged area

510. The ability of crop plants to grow, develop and reproduce normally under moisture deficit condition is referred to as
    a) Salinity resistance b) Drought resistance
    c) Alkalinity resistance d) All of the above

511. Improvement in the drought tolerance ability of a plant is known as
    a) Drought tolerance b) Drought escape
    c) Drought resistance d) Drought hardening

512. The instrument, Lysimeter is used to measure the
    a) Stomatal appratus b) Tissue water potential
    c) Slat tolerance d) Rate of photosynthesis

513. The instrument, psychrometer is used to measure the
    a) Stomatal appratus b) Tissue water potential
    c) Slat tolerance d) Rate of photosynthesis

514. The drought is measured in terms of
    a) Yield performance b) Leaf water retention
    c) Photosynthesis d) All of the above

515. The instrument, porometer used to measure the
    a) Stomatal appratus b) Tissue water potential
    c) Slat tolerance d) Rate of photosynthesis

516. The level of different chemicals increase in drought conditions are
    a) Abscisic acid b) Proline
    c) Ethylene d) All of the above

517. The indication of drought with respect to plant morphological features are
    a) Leaf rolling b) Deep root system
    c) Both A and B d) Increase in proline level

518. The indication of drought with respect to biochemical feature is

a) Increase in proline level b) Deep root system

c) Leaf rolling d) All of the above

519. The drought tolerance is associated with

a) Deep root system

b) Waxy and small leaves

c) Small and less number of stomata

d) All of the above

520. The plants can grow normally under excessive moisture condition are called as

a) Hydrophyte b) Xerophyte

c) Glycophyte d) Sociophyte

521. The plants which are very sensitive to high salt concentration are known as

a) Hydrophyte b) Xerophyte

c) Glycophyte d) Sociophyte

522. The plants which can grow normally on hills are called as

a) Hydrophyte b) Xerophyte

c) Lithophyte d) Sociophyte

523. The plants can grow normally under shade conditions are referred to as

a) Hydrophyte b) Xerophyte

c) Glycophyte d) Sociophyte

524. The plant which can grown normally under saline conditions are called as

a) Hydrophyte b) Halophyte

c) Lithophyte d) Sociophyte

525. The plant which can grow normally under acidic soil are called as

a) Hydrophyte b) Halophyte

c) Lithophyte d) Oxylophyte

526. The plants can grow normally under moisture deficit condition are called as

a) Xerophyte b) Halophyte

c) Lithophyte d) Oxylophyte

527. The ability of plants to maintain favorable internal water balance under moisture stress is called as

a) Drought avoidance b) Drought tolerance

c) Drought hardening d) Drought escape

528. The ability of crop plants to grow, develop and reproduce normally under moisture deficit condition is called as

a) Drought avoidance b) Drought tolerance

c) Drought hardening d) Drought escape

529. The drought resistance mechanisms are

a) Drought escape and avoidance

b) Drought resistance

c) Drought tolerance

d) All of the above

530. The simplest way to survive the crop plants from drought condition is

a) Use balanced NPK b) Use early varieties

c) Changed the planting sites d) All of the above

531. Drought avoidance mechanisms are

a) Which reduce water loss through transpiration

b) Which maintain water uptake during drought period

c) Higher photosynthesis

d) Both A and B

532. Drought avoidance leads

a) Reeducation in photosynthesis

b) Increase in root development

c) Reduction in the growth of aerial parts

d) All of the above

533. In cereals, the drought avoidance mechanism operates during

a) Vegetative phase b) Reproductive phase
c) Seedling stage d) All of the above

534. In cereals, the drought tolerance mechanism operates during

a) Vegetative phase b) Reproductive phase
c) Seedling stage d) All of the above

535. Earliness in many crops is a desirable character which leads to

a) Drought escape b) Drought tolerance
c) Drought resistance d) All of the above

536. The leaf water status and stomatal activities are measured by

a) Infrared thermometer b) Psychrometer
c) Porometer d) Lysimeter

537. In plants. Leaves with closed stomata will exhibit

a) Higher temperature b) Lower temperature
c) Both A and B d) None of the above

538. Leaves with open stomata have cooling effect due to

a) Water loss through evaporation
b) Water loss through photosynthesis
c) Water loss through transpiration
d) All of the above

539. In India, breeding work for salt resistance is carried out at

a) IARI, New Delhi b) NBPGR, New Delhi
c) CSSRI, Karnal d) PAU, Ludhiana

540. Abscisic acid promotes

a) Leaf senescence b) Tillering
c) Fruit ripening d) All of the above

541. The hormone called as stress hormone is

a) Abscisic acid b) Auxin
c) Cytokinine d) Gibberellins

542. The approximate arable geographical area of the world is
    a) 33.2%   b) 21.4%
    c) 25.2%   d) 26.8%

543. The geographical area of the world under cultivation is
    a) 12.1%   b) 10.4%
    c) 10.2%   d) 14.6%

544. The approximate arable geographical area in India is
    a) 12.3%   b) 13.6%
    c) 11.3%   d) 22.6%

545. Due to abiotic stresses, the total per cent reduction in crop yields is
    a) 80%   b) 55%
    c) 70%   d) 45%

546. The DUS refers to
    a) Distinctiveness   b) Uniformity
    c) Stability   d) All of the above

547. The NDUS refers to
    a) Novelty and Distinctiveness
    b) Uniformity
    c) Stability
    d) All of the above

548. Al the released as well as notified varieties are called as
    a) Farmer's variety   b) Example variety
    c) Reference variety   d) Extant variety

549. A variety can give constant performance after repeated reproduction is called as
    a) Stability   b) Novelty
    c) Uniformity   d) Distinctiveness

550. A new variety which has to be registered under PVP act is called as

a) Candidate variety b) Example variety

c) Reference variety d) Extant variety

551. PVP act was initially acted in country

a) Russia b) USA

c) Japan d) Canada

552. World seed year was declared in

a) 1951 b) 1971

c) 1961 d) 1981

553. The UPOV (Union for Protection of New Plant Varieties) was constituted in the year

a) 1951 b) 1971

c) 1961 d) 1981

554. The first UPOV convention was held in

a) Paris, 1951 b) USA, 1951

c) Paris, 1961 d) USA, 1961

555. The first UPOV Act formulated in year

a) 1976 b) 1988

c) 1978 d) 1986

556. UPOV Act (1978) was revised in year

a) 1991 b) 2001

c) 1998 d) 1995

557. The PPVFR Act was enacted from

a) 1991 b) 2001

c) 1998 d) 1995

558. According to UPOV Act (1978), the requirement of protection were

a) Stability b) Distinctiveness

c) Uniformity d) All of the above

559. According to UPOV Act (1991), the requirement of protection were
  a) Stability
  b) Novelty and Distinctiveness
  c) Uniformity
  d) All of the above

560. Under the PPVFR Act (2001), the requirement of protection were
  a) Stability
  b) Novelty and Distinctiveness
  c) Uniformity
  d) All of the above

561. According to UPOV Act (1978), the duration of protection were
  a) Minimum 15 year b) Minimum 25 years
  c) Minimum 20 years d) None of the above

562. According to UPOV Act (1991), the duration of protection were
  a) Minimum 15 year b) Minimum 25 years
  c) Minimum 20 years d) None of the above

563. Under PPVFR Act (2001), the duration of protection for extent and new varieties were
  a) Minimum 15 year b) Minimum 25 years
  c) Minimum 20 years d) None of the above

564. Under PPVFR Act (2001), the duration of protection for tree and vine varieties were
  a) Minimum 15 year b) Minimum 25 years
  c) Minimum 20 years d) Minimum 18 years

565. The headquarters of UPOV is located at
  a) Maxico b) London
  c) Geneva d) USA

566. The period of protection for fruit crops under UPOV Act (1978) is

a) Minimum 15 year
b) Minimum 25 years
c) Minimum 20 years
d) Minimum 18 years

567. The period of protection for fruit crops under UPOV Act (1991) is

a) Minimum 15 year
b) Minimum 25 years
c) Minimum 20 years
d) Minimum 18 years

568. The UPOV act was enacted in India,

a) In January, 2004
b) In January, 2006
c) In January, 2002
d) In January, 2008

569. Plant Variety Protection Act permits protection of

a) Parents of hybrids
b) Hybrids
c) Varieties
d) All of the above

570. PVP Act protects the kinds of hybrids were

a) Single cross hybrid
b) Three way cross hybrid
c) Double cross hybrid
d) All of the above

571. Under PVP Act, the crops were protected like

a) Fruit crops
b) Tree crops
c) Vine crops
d) All of the above

572. The Intellectual Property Rights (IPR) like patents, Trademarks, Trade names, Domine names were included in

a) Primary rights
b) Sui Generis rights
c) Both (a) and (b)
d) None of the above

573. Under IPR, which one is sui generis rights

a) Copyrights
b) PBR
c) GI
d) Trade secrets

574. Farmer's right comes under

a) Primary rights
b) Sui Generis rights
c) Both (a) and (b)
d) None of the above

575. Under database rights, the period of protection is

a) Minimum 15 year b) Minimum 25 years
c) Minimum 20 years d) None of the above

576. Under copyrights, the period of protection is

a) Minimum 15 year b) Minimum 25 years
c) Minimum 20 years d) 70-120 years

577. The term Supplementary Protection Certificate (SPC) is used in

a) Asian countries b) European countries
c) African countries d) American countries

578. The Supplementary Protection Certificate (SPC) rights is available for

a) Drugs b) Insecticides
c) Herbicides d) All of the above

579. Improved seed results in

a) Better germination b) Vigorous seedling growth
c) Higher crop stand d) All of the above

580. The condition in which the anthers and stigma of a bisexual flower mature at the same time is known as

a) Cleistogamy b) Heterogamy
c) Syngamy d) Homogamy

581. Causes of deterioration of a variety is

a) Mendelian variation b) Mechanical admixture
c) Mutation only d) All of the above

582. Land races refers to

a) Primitive cultivars b) Modern cultivars
c) Obsolate cultivars d) None of the above

583. The sum total of unfavourable genes is known as

a) Gene pool b) Genetic advance
c) Genetic load d) All of the above

584. Reduction or loss in vigour and fertility as a result of inbreeding is

a) Heterosis b) Inbreeding depression
c) Hybrid vigour d) None of the above

585. Vertical resistance can be exploited through

a) Development of multilines b) Gene pyramiding
c) Gene deployment d) All of the above

586. In plants, resistant genes for disease and insect resistance are used from

a) Cultivated varieties b) Mutations
c) Wild varieties d) All of the above

587. Disease and insect resistance is governed by

a) Oligogenes b) Plasma genes
c) Polygenes d) All of the above

588. Horizontal resistance is also referred as

a) Minor gene resistance b) Polygenic resistance
c) General resistance d) All of the above

589. Vertical resistance is known as

a) Major gene resistance b) Oligogenic resistance
c) Race specific resistance d) All of the above

590. Distant hybridization is associated with

a) Cross incompatibility b) Hybrid breakdown
c) Hybrid inviability d) All of the above

591. Outbreeding leads to reduction in

a) Homozygosity b) Population mean
c) Heterozygosity d) All of the above

592. Inbreeding of cross pollinated species leads to increase in

a) Homozygosity b) Population mean
c) Heterozygosity d) All of the above

593. The term useful heterosis was first used by
   a) Shull (1914)
   b) Meredith and Bridge (1972)
   c) Hull (1950)
   d) Simmonds (1979)

594. Single cross hybrids are used in
   a) Development of three way cross hybrids
   b) Prediction of double cross performance
   c) Development of double cross hybrids
   d) All of the above

595. Highest adaptability is observed in
   a) Single cross   b) Three way cross
   c) Double cross   d) Multiple cross

596. Heterobeltiosis is estimated over the
   a) Mid parent   b) Popular hybrid
   c) Popular variety   d) Better parent

597. Highest uniformity is observed in
   a) Single cross   b) Double cross
   c) Three way cross   d) Multiple cross

598. Hybrid progeny from a cross between two inbreds is known as
   a) Single cross hybrid   b) Three way cross hybrid
   c) Double cross hybrid   d) Multi cross hybrid

599. Heterosis over the best commercial variety is referred as
   a) Mean heterosis   b) Useful heterosis
   c) Heterobeltiosis   d) None of the above

600. Heterosis can be fixed by
   a) Asexual reproduction   b) Polyploidy
   c) Apomixis   d) All of the above

Answer Key

1. **c**	2. **a**	3. **b**	4. **a**	5. **a**	6. **a**	7. **c**	8. **b**
9. **c**	10. **a**	11. **d**	12. **d**	13. **b**	14. **a**	15. **b**	16. **d**
17. **c**	18. **b**	19. **a**	20. **d**	21. **a**	22. **a**	23. **b**	24. **a**
25. **a**	26. **c**	27. **a**	28. **b**	29. **d**	30. **c**	31. **b**	32. **b**
33. **c**	34. **c**	35. **c**	36. **b**	37. **d**	38. **d**	39. **c**	40. **a**
41. **c**	42. **b**	43. **a**	44. **d**	45. **a**	46. **d**	47. **d**	48. **a**
49. **c**	50. **d**	51. **a**	52. **c**	53. **b**	54. **a**	55. **d**	56. **c**
57. **b**	58. **a**	59. **c**	60. **b**	61. **d**	62. **a**	63. **c**	64. **c**
65. **d**	66. **a**	67. **b**	68. **d**	69. **b**	70. **d**	71. **c**	72. **b**
73. **c**	74. **d**	75. **d**	76. **a**	77. **a**	78. **c**	79. **d**	80. **d**
81. **c**	82. **d**	83. **d**	84. **c**	85. **b**	86. **b**	87. **b**	88. **d**
89. **a**	90. **c**	91. **c**	92. **a**	93. **a**	94. **a**	95. **a**	96. **b**
97. **a**	98. **c**	99. **c**	100. **b**	101. **d**	102. **c**	103. **d**	104. **a**
105. **c**	106. **c**	107. **c**	108. **a**	109. **c**	110. **d**	111. **a**	112. **b**
113. **b**	114. **c**	115. **c**	116. **a**	117. **d**	118. **a**	119. **a**	120. **b**
121. **c**	122. **b**	123. **d**	124. **d**	125. **a**	126. **d**	127. **b**	128. **c**
129. **b**	130. **c**	131. **a**	132. **c**	133. **a**	134. **a**	135. **c**	136. **c**
137. **a**	138. **d**	139. **a**	140. **a**	141. **c**	142. **d**	143. **c**	144. **a**
145. **c**	146. **d**	147. **a**	148. **c**	149. **d**	150. **b**	151. **a**	152. **c**
153. **c**	154. **a**	155. **b**	156. **b**	157. **b**	158. **c**	159. **c**	160. **d**
161. **d**	162. **d**	163. **a**	164. **a**	165. **a**	166. **c**	167. **b**	168. **c**
169. **b**	170. **c**	171. **a**	172. **b**	173. **a**	174. **b**	175. **b**	176. **d**
177. **a**	178. **d**	179. **a**	180. **a**	181. **d**	182. **d**	183. **b**	184. **a**
185. **a**	186. **a**	187. **d**	188. **d**	189. **a**	190. **d**	191. **a**	192. **a**
193. **a**	194. **d**	195. **d**	196. **d**	197. **b**	198. **c**	199. **a**	200. **c**
201. **d**	202. **c**	203. **d**	204. **d**	205. **b**	206. **d**	207. **c**	208. **a**
209. **a**	210. **b**	211. **c**	212. **d**	213. **c**	214. **a**	215. **a**	216. **b**
217. **c**	218. **c**	219. **a**	220. **a**	221. **b**	222. **d**	223. **b**	224. **d**
225. **d**	226. **d**	227. **a**	228. **d**	229. **b**	230. **c**	231. **d**	232. **c**

233. **b** 234. **c** 235. **d** 236. **a** 237. **c** 238. **a** 239. **b** 240. **a**
241. **b** 242. **a** 243. **b** 244. **c** 245. **b** 246. **c** 247. **c** 248. **c**
249. **c** 250. **d** 251. **b** 252. **d** 253. **a** 254. **d** 255. **d** 256. **d**
257. **d** 258. **c** 259. **a** 260. **d** 261. **a** 262. **c** 263. **d** 264. **b**
265. **a** 266. **d** 267. **c** 268. **c** 269. **c** 270. **b** 271. **d** 272. **d**
273. **c** 274. **b** 275. **c** 276. **b** 277. **a** 278. **a** 279. **c** 280. **b**
281. **b** 282. **c** 283. **b** 284. **a** 285. **b** 286. **a** 287. **d** 288. **c**
289. **c** 290. **a** 291. **c** 292. **a** 293. **d** 294. **c** 295. **d** 296. **c**
297. **a** 298. **a** 299. **d** 300. **c** 301. **b** 302. **b** 303. **a** 304. **b**
305. **c** 306. **a** 307. **d** 308. **d** 309. **b** 310. **d** 311. **a** 312. **b**
313. **c** 314. **d** 315. **b** 316. **d** 317. **a** 318. **c** 319. **a** 320. **b**
321. **b** 322. **a** 323. **d** 324. **c** 325. **b** 326. **a** 327. **c** 328. **a**
329. **b** 330. **a** 331. **b** 332. **d** 333. **d** 334. **a** 335. **d** 336. **b**
337. **a** 338. **a** 339. **c** 340. **d** 341. **b** 342. **c** 343. **c** 344. **d**
345. **b** 346. **d** 347. **d** 348. **c** 349. **d** 350. **a** 351. **c** 352. **c**
353. **b** 354. **d** 355. **c** 356. **c** 357. **b** 358. **d** 359. **b** 360. **d**
361. **d** 362. **b** 363. **d** 364. **c** 365. **c** 366. **c** 367. **c** 368. **a**
369. **d** 370. **d** 371. **b** 372. **a** 373. **c** 374. **a** 375. **b** 376. **a**
377. **d** 378. **a** 379. **d** 380. **d** 381. **a** 382. **b** 383. **c** 384. **b**
385. **c** 386. **c** 387. **d** 388. **d** 389. **d** 390. **a** 391. **d** 392. **a**
393. **c** 394. **b** 395. **a** 396. **b** 397. **a** 398. **d** 399. **d** 400. **d**
401. **a** 402. **c** 403. **d** 404. **c** 405. **a** 406. **c** 407. **b** 408. **d**
409. **c** 410. **a** 411. **c** 412. **c** 413. **c** 414. **c** 415. **d** 416. **d**
417. **c** 418. **a** 419. **b** 420. **d** 421. **d** 422. **d** 423. **a** 424. **c**
425. **b** 426. **b** 427. **d** 428. **d** 429. **b** 430. **d** 431. **a** 432. **a**
433. **c** 434. **b** 435. **d** 436. **b** 437. **c** 438. **b** 439. **d** 440. **a**
441. **d** 442. **d** 443. **d** 444. **c** 445. **a** 446. **c** 447. **d** 448. **c**
449. **d** 450. **d** 451. **a** 452. **c** 453. **d** 454. **b** 455. **a** 456. **a**
457. **c** 458. **a** 459. **a** 460. **d** 461. **b** 462. **a** 463. **b** 464. **c**
465. **b** 466. **d** 467. **a** 468. **c** 469. **d** 470. **b** 471. **c** 472. **d**

473. **a**	474. **d**	475. **a**	476. **c**	477. **c**	478. **b**	479. **c**	480. **d**
481. **c**	482. **c**	483. **d**	484. **b**	485. **a**	486. **c**	487. **b**	488. **b**
489. **c**	490. **a**	491. **c**	492. **b**	493. **d**	494. **b**	495. **b**	496. **d**
497. **d**	498. **d**	499. **a**	500. **a**	501. **c**	502. **b**	503. **a**	504. **a**
505. **c**	506. **d**	507. **a**	508. **d**	509. **a**	510. **b**	511. **d**	512. **c**
513. **b**	514. **d**	515. **a**	516. **d**	517. **c**	518. **a**	519. **d**	520. **a**
521. **c**	522. **c**	523. **d**	524. **b**	525. **d**	526. **a**	527. **a**	528. **b**
529. **d**	530. **b**	531. **d**	532. **d**	533. **a**	534. **b**	535. **a**	536. **a**
537. **a**	538. **c**	539. **c**	540. **a**	541. **a**	542. **b**	543. **d**	544. **c**
545. **b**	546. **d**	547. **d**	548. **d**	549. **a**	550. **a**	551. **b**	552. **c**
553. **c**	554. **c**	555. **c**	556. **a**	557. **b**	558. **d**	559. **d**	560. **d**
561. **a**	562. **c**	563. **a**	564. **d**	565. **c**	566. **d**	567. **b**	568. **b**
569. **d**	570. **d**	571. **d**	572. **a**	573. **b**	574. **b**	575. **a**	576. **d**
577. **b**	578. **d**	579. **d**	580. **c**	581. **d**	582. **a**	583. **c**	584. **b**
585. **d**	586. **d**	587. **d**	588. **d**	589. **d**	590. **d**	591. **c**	592. **a**
593. **b**	594. **d**	595. **d**	596. **d**	597. **a**	598. **a**	599. **b**	600. **d**

7

Basic Concepts in Biotechnology /Principles of Biotechnology

1. Taq polymerase usually adds which nucleotide at the end of the polymerized strand of DNA

   a) Adenine c) Cytosine

   b) Guanine d) Thimine

2. Nucleic acid was first discovered as nuclein by

   a) A. Cornberg c) H.G.Khorana

   b) J.Griffith d) F.Meischer

3. Building blocks of nucleic acids are.

   a) Amino Acid c) Nucleotides

   b) Nucleoproteins d) Nucleosides

4. Who among the following established that RNA is genetic material ?

   a) Fraenkal-Conorat c) Nirenberg and Holley

   b) Griffith d) Lederberg

5. Watson and Crick are known for their discover that DNA.

   a) Is single stranded helix c) Is a double stranded helix

   b) Contain deoxyribose only d) Synthesizes r-RNA

6. Watson and Crick proposed the model of DNA Structure in.

   a) 1953 c) 1963

   b) 1943 d) 1955

7. DNA is present in
   a) Nucleolus
   b) Plasma membrane
   c) Mitochondria
   d) Both A and C
8. In DNA, the Sugar is
   a) Deoxy ribose
   b) Ribose
   c) Cellulose
   d) Arabinose
9. DNA is found in
   a) Chromatin
   b) Nucleus
   c) Nucleolus
   d) Cytoplasm
10. A nucleoside is the combination of
   a) Sugar and Nitrogen base
   b) Sugar, Phosphate and Nitrogen base
   c) Nitrogen base and Phosphate
   d) Nitrogen base, Phosphate and water
11 Ribose is a
   a) Monosaccharide
   b) Disaccharide
   c) Polysaccharide
   d) Non of the above
12. A Riboside is a
   a) Ribose+Phosphate+base
   b) Ribose+base
   c) Ribose+Phosphate
   d) Base+Phosphate
13. DNA contains
   a) Five carbon sugar
   b) Six carbon sugar
   c) Four carbon sugar
   d) Chain of nucleosides
14. Single stranded DNA molecules are found in
   a) Tabacco mosaic virus (TMV)
   b) Rous sarcoma virus
   c) Small pox virus
   d) x x 174

15. DNA generally acts a template for the synthesis of

a) Only protein
c) Only RNA
b) Only DNA
d) Both DNA and RNA

16. The replication of DNA is

a) Conservative and continuous
b) Semi-conservative and non-continuous
c) Semi-conservative and semi-continuous
d) Semi-conservative and continuous

17. Synthesis of DNA takes place by

a) Transduction
c) Transformation
b) Transcription
d) Replication

18. DNA differs from RNA

a) In the nature of sugar alone
b) In the nature of purines alone
c) In the nature of pyrimidines alone
d) In the nature of sugar and pyrimidine

19. Primary difference between RNA DNA is that the former

a) Contains thymine
b) Contains uracil
c) Contains fewer oxygen atoms
d) Lacks adenine

20. The similarity between RNA and DNA is that

a) Are double stranded
b) Have similar sugar
c) Are polymers of nucleotides
d) Have similar pyrimidines

21. Difference of RNA from DNA is in the

a) Pentose sugar
c) Pyrimidine
b) Purine
d) Nucleotides

22. The two strands of DNA are bound by
    a) Phosphate-diester bonds
    b) Covalent bonds
    c) Hydrogen bonds
    d) Ionic bonds
23. The scientist who first synthesized the DNA *in vitro* was
    a) A.Kornberg
    b) A.Garrod
    c) J.D.Watson
    d) H.G.khorana
24. The diameter of DNA molecule is
    a) 50 &
    b) 20 &
    c) 100 &
    d) 200 &
25. If the base sequence in one polynucleotide series of DNA is G-C-A-T-G, what shall be the sequence in the replicated complementary strand?
    a) G-C-A-T-G
    b) C-G-T-A-C
    c) A-T-G-C-G
    d) G-C-A-T-C
26. Adenine is the kind of
    a) Purine
    b) Pyrimidine
    c) Phosphate
    d) Amino acids
27. The Nitrogen bases in DNA are
    a) AUGC
    b) UTGC
    c) ATGC
    d) ATUC
28. In DNA, guanine pairs with
    a) Cytosine
    b) Thimine
    c) Uracil
    d) Adenine
29. Purine Basis of DNA are
    a) Uracil and adenine
    b) Guanine and adenine
    c) Adenine and cyticine
    d) None of the above
30. The C-value of DNA refers to
    a) Total amount of DNA per haploid genome
    b) Total amount of DNA per somatic cell
    c) Amount of DNA present in heterosomes
    d) Amount of DNA present in autosomes

31. Denaturation of DNA molecule depends upon

a) Purine contents
c) A + T contents
b) Pyrimidine contents
d) G + C contents

32. Which of the following chemicals can be intercalated in between the nucleotides of DNA?

a) Ethidium bromide
c) Ethyl bromide
b) Potassium iodide
d) Indole 3 Acetic Acid

33. The topoisomerases are responsible for the following in the DNA molecule

a) Denaturing
c) Supercoiling
b) Annealing
d) Relaxation while uncoiling

34. Those enzymes which break specific nucleotide sequences are precisely called as

a) Nucleases
c) Exonucleases
b) Endonucleases
d) Restriction enzymes

35. The replicating units of DNA of a chromosome are called as

a) Replicons
c) Okazaki units
b) Okazaki pieces
d) Palindromes

36. The proteins which unwinds DNA molecule during replication are called as

a) Topoisomerases
c) Swiveling proteins
b) Helicases
d) Primases

37. During DNA replication the term 'leading strand' is applied to the one which always replicates in

a) 5' → 3' direction continuously
c) 3' → 5' direction continuously
b) 5' → 3' direction discontinuously
d) 3' → 5' direction discontinuously

38. An enzyme which forms the RNA primer during DNA replication is designated as

a) Isomerase c) Nuclease

b) Replicase d) Primase

39. The superhelix relaxing protein has been also called as

a) SSB c) Both

b) ω d) None

40. The DNA polymerizing enzyme was discovered by

a) Crick c) Wilkins

b) Kornberg d) Cairn

41. Which polymersing enzyme is concerned with DNA repair in higher plants?

a) Polymerase I c) γ – Polymerase I

b) Polymerase III d) β Polymerase

42. Which of the following is the main polymerizing enzyme?

A. Polymerase III c) Polymerase

b) γ – Polymerase d) None of these

43. The okazaki pieces of DNA are joined by the enzyme

a) Polymerase c) Primases

b) Polynucleotide ligase d) Primsomes

44. The length of one pitch or C – DNA is approximately

a) 1.28 & c) 3.33 &

b) 2.24 & d) 4.31 &

45. The number of base pairs per turn of helix in Z – DNA is

a) 10 c) 11

b) 12 d) 9.33

46. The formation of m – RNA from DNA is called

a) Translation c) Transduction

b) Transformation d) Transcription

47. RNA is synthesized by DNA in the
    a) Nucleus
    b) Enzymes
    c) Cytoplasm
    d) Chromosomes

48. The process of transcription is involved in the
    a) Conversion of RNA into DNA
    b) Movement of RNA from nucleus to ribosome
    c) Change of one form of RNA into another
    d) Formation of RNA from DNA

49. The function of t - RNA is
    a) Selection of amino acids
    b) Production of m RNA
    c) Production of ribosomes
    d) Production of mircosomes

50. Adenine in RNA will pair with
    a) Thymine
    b) Cytosine
    c) Guanine
    d) Uracil

51. Translation is the process when
    a) Replication of DNA takes place
    b) Messenger RNA is formed from DNA
    c) Golgi bodies are formed
    d) Protein synthesis takes place at the site of ribosomes

52. If the base sequence of the strand of DNA is CAT TAG CAT GAT GAC. What will be sequence of the RNA strand which is complementary with the DNA.
    a) GTA ATC GAT GTA CTA
    b) GUAAUC GUA GUA CUG
    c) GTA ATG ATG GUA CUG
    d) Data insufficient

53. The messenger RNA is formed
    a) From DNA in the nucleus
    b) In the cytoplasm
    c) From the ribosomes on ER
    d) By free ribosomes

54. RNA controls the synthesis of
    a) Amino acids
    b) Nucleotides
    c) Chromosomes
    d) Enzymes

55. The principal function of m RNA molecule is to
    a) Manufacture new ribosomes
    b) Synthesize new DNA molecule
    c) Convert DNA molecule to molecule of RNA
    d) Act as a template for synthesis of proteins

56. RNA is absent in
    a) Plasma membrane
    b) Cytoplasm
    c) Chromosome
    d) Ribosome

57. The function of nucleolus is the synthesis of
    a) DNA
    b) m-RNA
    c) r-RNA
    d) t-RNA

58. Who was awarded Nobel prize for the synthesis of RNA in 1959?
    a) S. Ochoa
    b) A. Kornberg
    c) H. Khorana
    d) Nirenberg

59. The purines of RNA are
    a) Uracil and guanine
    b) Guanine and adenine
    c) Adenine and cytosine
    d) Uracil and thymine

60. Which of the following is the smallest RNA?
    a) Messenger RNA
    b) Ribosomal RNA
    c) Transfer RNA
    d) Chromosomal RNA

61. Which of the following has a clover leaf shaped structure?
    a) t RNA
    b) r RNA
    c) m RNA
    d) DNA

62. Through which enzyme can RNA give rise to DNA?
    a) Restriction enzyme
    b) DNA polymerase
    c) RNA polymerase
    d) Reverse trancriptase

63. The smallest RNA fraction present in ribosomes has a sedimentation coefficient around.
    a) 5.8 S
    b) 5 S
    c) 3.8 S
    d) 8 S

64. Mark the correct statement.
   a) Eukaryotic m-RNA is monocistronic
   b) Eukaryotic m-RNA is polycistronic
   c) Both the m-RNA are monocistronic
   d) Both the m-RNA are polycistronic

65. Mark the correct statement
   a) Prokaryotic m-RNA undergoes processing
   b) Eukaryotic m-RNA undergoes processing
   c) Bothe the m-RNA undergo processing
   d) No m-RNA undergoes processing

66. The prokaryotic m-RNA has
   a) Poly A tails at 5' end
   c) Poly A tails at both ends
   b) Poly A tails at 3' end
   d) No poly A tail

67. The eukaryotic m-RNA has
   a) Poly A tail 5'end
   b) Poly A tail at 3' end
   c) Poly A tails at both the ends
   d) No poly A tail

68. The initiating codon in m-RNA's coding region is
   a) AUC
   c) AUG
   b) CCG
   d) CUG

69. The eukaryotic genes are interrupted by non coding segment called
   a) Exons
   c) Linker DNA
   b) Introns
   d) Intercistron

70. The total percentage of t-RNA in a cell ranges between
   a) 25-30
   c) 10-20
   b) 20-25
   d) 5-10

71. The person who received a Nobel prize for describing the molecular structure of t-RNA

a) Nirenberg
c) Ochoa
b) Khorana
d) Holley

72. The Greek letter Ødenotes the following nitrogen base in t-RNA

a) Pseudouridine
c) Dihydrouridine
b) Inosine
d) None of these

73. The variable arm of yeast's alanine t-RNA is made up of

a) 20-31 bases
c) 32-55 bases
b) 3-20 bases
d) 45-60 bases

74. Due to further bonding, the clover leaf structure of t-RNA assumes a tertiary form that appears

a) T-shaped
c) X-shaped
b) L-shaped
d) S-shaped

75. The 3' end of a t-RNA always terminates with the bases

a) G-G-A
c) C-A-C
b) A-C-C
d) C-C-A

76. The viroids are

a) Linear double stranded RNA strands
b) Linear single stranded RNA strands
c) Double stranded RNA circles
d) Single stranded RNA circles

77. The stem of anticodonal arm is made up of

a) 3 to 4 bases
c) 8 bases
b) 5 to 7 bases
d) 12 bases

78. The 5' end of a t-RNA always starts with the base

a) Adenine
c) Guanine
b) Cytosine
d) Uracil

79. The total number of essential amino acids in the living being is
   a) Fifteen
   b) Twenty
   c) Twenty two
   d) Eight

80. The Nobel prize for cracking the genetic code was given to
   a) Nirenberg and Khorana
   b) Nirenberg and Holley
   c) All of these
   d) Nirenberg

81. With adenine and cytosine only, how many different codons are possible?
   a) Eight
   b) Six
   c) Sixteen
   d) Four

82. The universal initiating codon is
   a) GUA
   b) UAG
   c) AUG
   d) AAG

83. When the synthesis of a protein begins, the following codon may also act as initiator
   a) UGU
   b) AUG
   c) AAG
   d) GUG

84. The codon that codes for the amino acid methionine is
   a) ACG
   b) AUG
   c) AAG
   d) AGG

85. How many codons code for the amino acid serine?
   a) Six
   b) Four
   c) Two
   d) Eight

86. The stop signals contain the following bases
   a) Adenine, guanine and cytosine
   b) Adenine, cytosine and uracil
   c) Uracil, guanine and adenine
   d) Any of these

87. The wobble concept was proposed by
   a) Watson and Crick
   b) Nirenberg and Leder
   c) Nirenberg and Matthaei
   d) Crick

88. The m-RNA AUGCAGGAUACG recognizes four amino acid and this character of the code refered to as
   a) Degeneracy
   b) Universality
   c) Nonambiguity
   d) Commalessness

89. According to wobble concept the G base in the anticodon can recognize the following base/s in the codon
   a) C only
   b) U or C
   c) A or C
   d) All of these

90. Which of the following is the missense mutation?
   a) UAC $\rightarrow$ UAG
   b) UGC $\rightarrow$ AUG
   c) Both of these
   d) AUU $\rightarrow$ AUC

91. Which of the following is the nonsense mutation?
   a) CUU $\rightarrow$ CUC
   b) CAU $\rightarrow$ GAC
   c) UGU $\rightarrow$ UGC
   d) None of these

92. The process by which protein are synthesized in a cell is called as.
   a) Transduction
   b) Translocation
   c) Transcription
   d) Translation

93. Gene is
   a) RNA molecule
   b) DNA molecule
   c) Protein molecule
   d) DNA + histone molecules

94. In cytoplasm, messenger RNA becomes attached to
   a) Mitochondria
   b) Chloroplast
   c) Ribosomes
   d) Centrosomes

95. The factor which determines the point of attachment of amino acid with t-RNA
   a) Amino acyl synthesis
   b) RNA Polymerase
   c) Sigma factor
   d) F_3 factor

96. During elongation of polypeptide chain (in translation), the sigma factor.

    a) Is release to again take part

    b) Is retain and it performs special function

    c) The function is not known

    d) Is used during the closing of chain

97. Wild type *E.coli* cells are growing in normal medium with glucose. They are transferred to a medium containing only lactose as the sugar. Which one of the following changes takes place?

    a) The *lac* operon is repressed

    b) All operons are induced

    c) *E.coli* cells stop dividing

    d) The lac operon is induced

98. The operon model of gene regulation and organization in prokaryotes was proposed by

    a) Jacob and monod

    b) Beadle and Tatum

    c) Messelson and Stahl

    d) Wilkins and Franklin

99. The lac operon is the example of

    a) Arabinose operon

    b) Inducible operon

    c) Repressible operon

    d) Ovelapping genes

100. Genes controls

    a) Heredity but not protein synthesis

    b) Protein synthesis but not heredity

    c) Protein synthesis and heredity

    d) Biochemical reaction of enzymes

Fill in the Blanks

1. The cap is formed in m-RNA due to condensation of ________ at 5' end

2. The formation of polypeptide chain constitutes the __________ structure of protein.

3. The three dimensional organization of protein molecule achieved by intramolecular bonding constitutes the __________ structure.

4. The path of the flow of genetic information has been termed as __________.

5. The enzyme RNA polymerase is made up of __________ polypeptides.

6. The heaviest component of RNA polymerase is __________.

7. The lightest component of RNA polymerase is __________.

8. The hnRNA is synthesized by the help of enzyme __________.

9. The sigma factor directs the RNA polymerase (holoenzyme) to bind with the __________ sequence.

10. The leading strand of DNA replication always proceeds in __________ direction.

11. The DNA molecule replicates in pieces called __________.

12. The RNA primer, during DNA replication synthesized by a special RNA polymerase called __________.

13. The enzyme __________ is meant for the replication of mitochondrial DNA in eukaryotes.

14. PCR was invented by __________

15. __________ is the example of imino acid.

Mark as True of False

1. More energy is required to break AT pairs than GC.

2. Enzyme endonucleases remove terminal nucleotides.

3. Structure of DNA was discovered by Watson and Crick

4. Cell without cell wall is known as cytoplasm

5. DNA is having negative charge
6. Callus is the differentiated mass of cell
7. RAPD is the example of dominant marker
8. Origin of replication in prokaryotes are known as *oriC*
9. Thermo stable *Taq* polymerase is isolated from bacterium strain *Bacillus thuringiensis*
10. Lipase enzyme is used for joining of two DNA sequences.
11. DNA polymerase provides negative super coiling for unwinding DNA helix during replication
12. Golden rice is transformed with orthologus genes from rice pant and *Bacillus spp.*
13. m-RNA is having poly-A tail at the 3' end
14. Flavor Savor tomato is engineered for the early ripening character.
15. Cry protein require alkaline pH for its activation

Match the followings

	GroupA	Answers	Group B
1.	DNA Replication	A.	*Bacillus Thuringiensis*
2.	Taq Man oligo Probes	B.	-CONH-
3.	Microsatellite	C.	β-Carotene
4.	RAPD	D.	Reverse transcriptase
5.	cDNA Synthesis	E.	Co-Dominant Marker
6.	Cry Protein	F.	Real Time PCR
7.	Golden Rice	G.	DNA polymerase
8.	Flavor Savor	H.	Herbicide Resistance Cotton
9.	Amino acid chain	I.	Dominant Marker
10.	Roundup ready	J.	Delayed Ripening

Answer Key

1.	**a**	2.	**d**	3.	**c**	4.	**a**	5.	**c**	6.	**a**	7.	**d**	8.	**a**
9.	**b**	10.	**a**	11.	**a**	12.	**b**	13.	**a**	14.	**d**	15.	**c**	16.	**b**
17.	**d**	18.	**a**	19.	**b**	20.	**c**	21.	**a**	22.	**c**	23.	**a**	24.	**b**
25.	**a**	26.	**a**	27.	**c**	28.	**a**	29.	**b**	30.	**a**	31.	**d**	32.	**a**
33.	**c**	34.	**d**	35.	**a**	36.	**b**	37.	**a**	38.	**d**	39.	**c**	40.	**b**
41.	**d**	42.	**a**	43.	**b**	44.	**d**	45.	**b**	46.	**d**	47.	**a**	48.	**d**
49.	**a**	50.	**d**	51.	**d**	52.	**b**	53.	**a**	54.	**d**	55.	**d**	56.	**a**
57.	**c**	58.	**a**	59.	**b**	60.	**c**	61.	**a**	62.	**d**	63.	**b**	64.	**a**
65.	**b**	66.	**d**	67.	**b**	68.	**c**	69.	**b**	70.	**c**	71.	**d**	72.	**a**
73.	**b**	74.	**b**	75.	**d**	76.	**d**	77.	**a**	78.	**c**	79.	**b**	80.	**d**
81.	**a**	82.	**c**	83.	**d**	84.	**b**	85.	**a**	86.	**c**	87.	**d**	88.	**d**
89.	**b**	90.	**d**	91.	**d**	92.	**d**	93.	**b**	94.	**c**	95.	**d**	96.	**a**
97.	**d**	98.	**a**	99.	**b**	100.	**c**								

Answers of the Blanks

1. Guanine
2. Primary
3. Tertiary
4. Central Dogma
5. Five
6. β (Beta)
7. ω (Omega)
8. RNA polymerase II or B
9. Promoter
10. 5' → 3'
11. Okazaki pieces
12. Primase
13. Gama (γ) - Polymerase
14. Kerry mullis
15. Proline

Answers of the True or False

1. False
2. False
3. True
4. False
5. True
6. False
7. True
8. True
9. False
10. False
11. False
12. False
13. True
14. False
15. True

Answers of the Match the followings

GroupA	GroupB
1.	G
2.	F
3.	E
4.	I
5.	D
6.	A
7.	C
8.	J
9.	B
10.	H

8

Plant Biochemistry and Biotechnology

1. They are bags of hydrolytic enzymes that bring about degradation of macromolecules
   a) Mitochondria
   b) Lysosomes
   c) Chloroplast
   d) Nucleus
2. What is the function of mitochondria?
   a) Generation of ATP
   b) To prepare foods
   c) In cell lyses
   d) None of the above
3. It is the mechanism by which cells internalize extracellular macromolecules
   a) Exocytosis
   b) Phagocytosis
   c) Endocytosis
   d) None of the above
4. Name the Sulfur containing amino acids.
   a) Valine and Glycin
   b) Phenylalanine and tyrosine.
   c) Histidine and proline
   d) Cysteine and methionine
5. Give the names of aromatic amino acids.
   a) Phenylalanine and tyrosine.
   b) Leucine and methionin
   c) Valine and Glycine
   d) Aspargin and glutamine

6. Give an example of an imino acid.
   a) Valine b) Histidine
   c) Proline d) Methionin
7. Benzene group is present in which amino acid?
   a) Histidin b) Glycin
   c) Phenyl alanine d) Prolin
8. The amino acid that cannot be synthesized in the body; and so, they are to be provided in the diet.
   a) Essential amino acids
   b) Non Essential amino acids
   c) Non necessary amino acids
   d) None of the above
9. How many amino acids are essential?
   a) 14 b) 12
   c) 10 d) 20
10. Which is an essential amino acid?
    a) phenyl alanine b) Arginine
    c) Serine d) proline
11. The pH at which the molecule carries no net charge is called
    a) Same pH b) Neutral pH
    c) Iso-electric point d) Neutral point
12. What are natural amino acids?
    a) D amino acids b) L amino acids
    c) Both A and B d) None of Above
13. Cupric ions in alkaline medium form a violet colour with peptide bond nitrogen.
    a) Xanthoproteic test b) Millon's test
    c) Molisch's test d) Biuret reaction
14. Will amino acids give a positive biuret test?
    a) No b) Yes
    c) Not predictable d) No Idea

15. Macromolecule made up by polymerisation of amino acids through peptide bonds

    a) Glycosides b) Cabohydrate

    c) Lipids d) Protein

16. How many peptide bonds are present in a tripeptide?

    a) 3 b) 4

    c) 2 d) 6

17. It denotes the number and sequence of amino acids in the protein.

    a) Primary structure b) Secondary structure

    c) Tertiary structure d) Quaternary structure

18. Sudden heritable changes in genetic makeup of individual called

    a) Recombination b) Evolution

    c) Replication d) Mutation

19. What is the function of oxido-reductases?

    a) Transfer of Hydrogen b) Transfer of H_2O

    c) Transfer of O_2 d) All of Above

20. What is the full form of NAD?

    a) Nicotinosine adenine dinucleotide

    b) Nicotinine adenine dinucleotide.

    c) Nicotinamide adenine dinucleotide

    d) Nicotinamide adenine diphosphate

21. That area (site) of the enzyme where catalysis occurs is referred to as

    a) Active site b) Action site

    c) Recognition site d) None of the above

22. Thermodynamically, the reaction in which energy is produced is classified?

    a) Endothermic reaction b) Exothermic reaction

    c) Iso therimc reaction d) None of the above

23. What is the immediate treatment for methanol poisoning?
    a) NaOH b) Methanol
    c) Acetone d) Ethanol

24. Enzymes whose concentration in a cell is independent of inducer are called
    a) Constitutive enzymes b) Indusible enzymes
    c) Both A and B d) None of the above

25. The term refers to the movement of charged particles through an electrolyte when subjected to an electric field
    a) Sothern blotting b) Chromatography
    c) Electroporation d) Electrophoresis

26. It is the ratio of the distance travelled by the substance (solute) to the distance travelled by the solvent.
    a) Rf value b) Rt value
    c) Rm value d) Rx value

27. Monosaccharides are combined together through
    a) Phosphate bond b) Peptide bond
    c) Glycosidic linkages d) None of the above

28. Name a few pentoses
    a) Arabinose, Xylose, Ribose
    b) Glucuse, fructose
    c) Arabinose, robose
    d) Galactose, xylose

29. Which isomer of carbohydrate is common in nature?
    a) L variety of sugar
    b) D variety of sugars
    c) Both A and B
    d) None of the above

30. Which is the most common monosaccharide in the body?
    a) Glucose b) Starch
    c) Sucrose d) Lactose

31. Which is the sugar found in milk?
    a) Maltose b) Lactose
    c) Fructose d) Sucrose
32. What is the reserve carbohydrate in plant kingdom?
    a) Cellulose b) Sucrose
    c) Glucose d) Starch
33. In this pathway, glucose is converted to pyruvate or lactate, along with production of a small quantity of energy
    a) Glycolysis b) Gluconeogenesis
    c) Glycogenolysis d) All of the above
34. In aerobic glycolysis, the net yield from one glucose molecule is how much?
    a) 12 ATP b) 2 ATP
    c) 8 ATP d) 38 ATP
35. During complete oxidation, what is the net yield of ATP from one glucose molecule?
    a) 8 ATP b) 12 ATP
    c) 2 ATP d) 38 ATP
36. How many ATPs are generated per one rotation of the citric acid cycle?
    a) 8 ATP b) 12 ATP
    c) 2 ATP d) 38 ATP
37. Pyruvate is converted to acetyl CoA by which enzyme?
    a) Pyruvate dehydrogenate
    b) Acetyl CoA synthetase
    c) Pyruvate Symthatase
    d) None of the above
38. What is the level of fasting blood sugar in a normal person?
    a) 120-150 mg/dl b) 40-70 mg/dl
    c) 70-110 mg/dl d) 150-210 mg/dl

39. Which one is the example of milk protein ?

a) Pepsin
b) Trypsin
c) Casein
d) Lectins

40. Where is insulin synthesised?

a) Pancreas
b) Stomach
c) Kidney
d) Heart

41. Which type of fatty acids is prevalent in human body?

a) Odd chain fatty acids
b) Even chain fatty acids
c) Both A and B
d) None of the above

42. How many carbon atoms are present in arachidonic acid?

a) 18 carbon
b) 16 carbon
c) 22 carbon
d) 20 carbon

43. What if full form of PUFA?

a) Poly Unused Fatty Acids
b) Poly Undigestible Fatty Acids
c) Poly Unsaturated Fatty Acids
d) Poly Unsaturated Free Fatty Acids

44. Which food stuffs contain cholesterol?

a) Non-vegetarian food
b) Vegetarian
c) Both A and B
d) No relation with food stuff

45. What is good cholesterol?

a) LDL cholesterol
b) HDL cholesterol
c) Both A and B
d) None of the above

46. Name polyunsaturated fatty acids
    a) Linoleic and linolenic acid
    b) Acetic acid and propionic acid
    c) Arachidic acid
    d) Palmitic acid
47. They act at one of the protein molecule, liberating amino acids sequentially, one at a time
    a) Exopeptidases b) Endopeptidases
    c) Both A and B d) None of the above
48. Lysine is deficient in which food stuffs?
    a) Pulses b) Cereals
    c) Both A and B d) None of the above
49. Which amino acid will give rise to a vitamin?
    a) Aspargine b) Histidine
    c) Tryptophan d) Glutamine
50. How many ATPs are generated per one rotation of the citric acid cycle?
    a) 12 ATP b) 8 ATP
    c) 2 ATP d) 38 ATP
51. How many ATP are produced in the oxidation of one molecule of NADH?
    a) Two b) Three
    c) Four d) Eight
52. How many ATP are produced in the oxidation of one molecule of FADH?
    a) Two b) Four
    c) Eight d) Thirty eight
53. The antigen binding capacity of immunoglobulin resides at which region of immunoglobulin?
    a) Constant region b) Variable region
    c) Both A & B d) None of the above

54. How many molecules of oxygen can bind with one hemoglobin?
a) Four b) Three
c) Two d) One

55. Why carbon monoxide becomes a poison?
a) Hb has more affinity to carbon monoxide than oxygen
b) Hb has more affinity to carbon dioxide than oxygen
c) Hb has les affinity to carbon monoxide than oxygen
d) Hb has less affinity to carbon monoxide than oxygen

56. What is the pro-Vitamin for Vitamin A?
a) Beta carotene present in plants
b) Alpha carotene
d) Vitamin B
d) None of the above

57. Nyctalopia is due to the deficiency of which Vitamin?
a) Vitamin D b) Vitamin C
c) Vitamin B d) Vitamin A

58. What is the function of Vitamin E ?
a) Anti-oxidant b) Anti Ageing
c) Both A and B d) None of the above

59. Beberi is due to the deficiency of which Vitamin?
a) Thiamine b) Vitamin B_6
c) Vitamin B_{12} d) Vitamin C

60. Pellagra is seen in the deficiency of which Vitamin?
a) Niacin b) Vitamin A
c) Vitamin B_6 d) Both A & C

61. What is the precursor of niacin?
a) Glycin b) Valine
c) Tryptophan d) Phenyl allanine

62. Which is the Vitamin totally absent in plant sources?
a) Vitamin B_{12} b) Vitamin A
c) Vitamin C d) Vitamin B_6

63. Which is the trace element, deficient in milk?
    a) Iron b) Mg
    c) Mn d) Zn
64. What is the calorific value of carbohydrates?
    a) Nine kilocalories per gram
    b) Four kilocalories per gram
    c) Two kilocalories per gram
    d) One kilocalories per gram
65. What is the calorific value of fats?
    a) Nine kilocalories per gram
    b) Four kilocalories per gram
    c) Two kilocalories per gram
    d) One kilocalories per gram
66. When pH falls by 1 unit, what is the change in the hydrogen ion concentration?
    a) Increases by 100 times b) Increases by 10 times
    c) Decreases by 100 times d) Decreases by 10 times
67. What is a nucleotide?
    a) Nitrogenous base + sugar
    b) Nitrogenous base + phosphate
    c) Nitrogenous base + sugar + phosphate
    d) None of the above
68. Name the common purines
    a) Adenine b) Cytosine
    c) Uracil d) Thymine
69. Which nitrogenous base is absent in DNA?
    a) Adenine b) Guanine
    c) Cytosine d) Uracil
70. Which base is found exclusively in DNA and not in RNA?
    a) Adenine b) Guanine
    c) Thymine d) Cytosine

71. What is relationship between the A+T and G+C contains of DNA.

a) A+T = G+C b) A+T > G+C

c) A+T < G+C d) No Relation

72. What are the enzymes required for DNA replication?

a) DNA polymerase b) Topo isomerase

c) DNA ligase d) All of the above

73. Replication is in which direction?

a) 5' to 3' b) 3' to 5'

c) Both directions d) None of the above

74. Which enzymes protect cellular ageing?

a) DNA polymerase b) RNA polymerase

c) Telomerase d) Reverse transcriptase

75. What is transcription?

a) The process of making a complementary mRNA copy of DNA

b) The process of making a DNA copy of DNA

c) The process of protein synthesis from RNA

d) None of the above

76. What is the initiating codon for protein synthesis?

a) UAA b) UAG

c) UGG d) AUG

77. Which enzyme is required for PCR (Polymerase Chain Reaction)?

a) RNA polymerase b) Reverse transcriptase

c) Taq polymerase d) All of the above

78. What is the causative organism of AIDS?

a) Human amino deficiency virus

b) Acquire immune deficiency virus

c) HIS

d) Human immunodeficiency virus

79. Lactose is made up of
a) Glucose + Galactose
b) Glucose + Fructose
c) Glucose + Glucose
d) None of the above

80. Who first synthesized urea in laboratory?
a) Kuhne
b) Lavoisier
c) Neuberg
d) Wohler

81. Red colour of tomato is due to the presence of
a) Anthrocynin
b) Chlorophyll
c) Lycopene
d) Tomatin

82. The toxin presence in young sorghum seedling
a) Steroid
b) Saponin
c) Hordin
d) Dhurrin

83. The flavor in onion and garlic is due to the presence of
a) Allyl propide
b) Lycopene
c) Garlic
d) Allyl sulphide

84. The organ of plant that exhibit negative geotropism
a) Stem
b) Root
c) Both
d) None

85. The immediate precuasor of gibbrelline
a) Ethylene
b) Aspartic Acid
c) Acetic Acid
d) Kaurene

86. The mass of undifferentiated cell is called as
a) Callus
b) Mass
c) Explants
d) Suspension

87. O_2 of photosynthesis come from
a) CO_2
b) Plants
c) H_2O
d) None

88. Embryo culture is helpful in
a) Recovery of distance hybrids
b) Propagation of orchids
c) Shortening of breeding cycle
d) All of the above

89. Cultivation of Apical Meristem as specially shoot Meristem is called

a) Embryo culture b) Pollen culture

c) Meristem culture d) Cell culture

90. Meristem culture is useful in

a) Vegetative propagation

b) Recovery of virus free stock

c) Germplasm conservation

d) All of the above

91. For obtaining haploid plants

a) Meristem culture b) Anther culture

c) Shoot tip culture d) None of above

92. 1 nm is equal to

a) 10^{-9} meter b) 10^{-9} cm

c) 10^{-9} um d) 100 A^0

93. In C_4 plants the initial acceptor of CO_2 is

a) Ribulose 1- 5 biphosphate

b) Phosphophenol puruvic acid

c) Both A and B

d) None of the above

94. Kreb cycle is also known as

a) Citric acid cycle b) Tricarboxylic cycle

c) Both A and B d) None of the above

95. Hormones that induce fruit ripening.

a) Ethylene b) Cytokinines

c) Auxins d) Gibberellins

96. The double helix structure of DNA was discovered by

a) Michaelis and Menten b) Berzelius

c) Meselson and Stahl d) Watson & Crick

97. The process of formation of complex substances from simple monomeric unit involving the energy is known as
    a) Catabolism b) Metabolism
    c) Anabolism d) All of the above

98. Who invented the PCR?
    a) Kary mullis b) Hargovind khurana
    c) Arber d) Kornberg

99. Name the trisaccharide
    a) Raffinose b) Stachyose
    c) Both A and B d) None of the above

100. Which is the most common gelling agent use in tissue culture
    a) Agar Agar b) Gum
    c) Agarose d) All of the ablove

Answer Key

1.	**b**	2.	**a**	3.	**c**	4.	**d**	5.	**a**	6.	**c**	7.	**c**	8.	**a**
9.	**c**	10.	**a**	11.	**c**	12.	**b**	13.	**d**	14.	**a**	15.	**d**	16.	**c**
17.	**a**	18.	**d**	19.	**a**	20.	**c**	21.	**a**	22.	**b**	23.	**d**	24.	**a**
25.	**d**	26.	**a**	27.	**c**	28.	**a**	29.	**b**	30.	**a**	31.	**b**	32.	**d**
33.	**a**	34.	**c**	35.	**d**	36.	**b**	37.	**a**	38.	**c**	39.	**c**	40.	**a**
41.	**b**	42.	**d**	43.	**c**	44.	**a**	45.	**b**	46.	**a**	47.	**a**	48.	**b**
49.	**c**	50.	**a**	51.	**b**	52.	**a**	53.	**b**	54.	**a**	55.	**a**	56.	**a**
57.	**d**	58.	**c**	59.	**a**	60.	**d**	61.	**c**	62.	**a**	63.	**a**	64.	**b**
65.	**a**	66.	**b**	67.	**c**	68.	**a**	69.	**d**	70.	**c**	71.	**a**	72.	**d**
73.	**a**	74.	**c**	75.	**a**	76.	**d**	77.	**c**	78.	**d**	79.	**a**	80.	**d**
81.	**c**	82.	**d**	83.	**d**	84.	**a**	85.	**d**	86.	**a**	87.	**c**	88.	**d**
89.	**c**	90.	**d**	91.	**b**	92.	**a**	93.	**b**	94.	**c**	95.	**a**	96.	**d**
97.	**c**	98.	**a**	99.	**c**	100.	**a**								

9

Bioinformatics in Agricultural Sciences: Introduction to Bioinformatics

1. The first researcher who sequence a whole genome, in 1977, was
   a) Todd Golub b) Frederick Sanger
   c) Craig Venter d) Stephen Fodor
2. The translated genes of genomes that encode proteins are referred as
   a) The open reading framc b) Introns
   c) Codons d) Pseudogenes
3. Of the organisms, what has the largest genome size?
   a) *Helicobacter pylori*
   b) *Drosophila melanogaster*
   c) *Saccharomyces cerevisiae*
   d) *Oryza sativa*
4. Genes for typical single-character Mendelian traits are called
   a) Segmental duplications b) Multigene families
   c) Tandem clusters d) Single-copy genes
5. The genes encoding rRNA are examples of
   a) Single-copy genes. b) Segmental duplications
   c) Tandem clusters of genes d) Multigene families

6. What type of noncoding DNA tends to be localized around the centromere?
   a) Constitutive heterochromatin
   b) Structural DNA
   c) Transposable elements
   d) Both a and b are correct
7. What type of transposon is most likely to cause a mutation?
   a) Retroposons
   b) LINES
   c) DNA transposons that copy themselves rather than RNA
   d) ALU transpositions
8. The transposons, that have lost their signals for replication are
   a) Long interspersed elements (lines)
   b) Dead transposons
   c) Parasitic elements
   d) ALU
9. The most efficient way to analyze variation at the genome level is
   a) Frequency of tandem clusters
   b) Number of transposons
   c) Single Nucleotide Polymorphisms (SNPs)
   d) Segmental duplications
10. The field of study involving the sequencing of the genomes is
    a) Molecular genetics b) Bioinformatics
    c) Genomics d) Taxonomy
11. Microarray gene chips can be used to
    a) Screen for mutations leading to cancer
    b) Identify carriers of genetic diseases
    c) Identify probable behavioral characters
    d) A, B, and C are Correct

12. The identification of the function of a gene in a genome can be carried out by
    a) Functional genomics b) Gene microarrays
    c) Bioinformatics d) Gel electrophoresis
13. Labeling a stretch of DNA according to its function is called
    a) Functional analysis b) Annotation
    c) Screening d) Promoting
14. The SWISS-PROT database was created by
    a) Departme nt of medical Biochemistry, University of Geneva
    b) European molecular Biology Laboratory (EMBL)
    c) Non of the Above
    d) Both of the Above
15. Transmissinon Control Protocol (TCP) was formulated by
    a) Bill Gates and Paul Allene
    b) Vint Cerf and Robert Khan
    c) Allan maxam, Walter Gilbert and Frederick Sanger
    d) Tom Truscott, Jim Ellis and Steve Bellovin
16. The aspects of Bioinformatics that are applied to drug discovery and drug designing are known as
    a) Pharmacoinformatics b) Biomedical Informatics
    c) Medical informatics d) All of the above
17. Which protocol is used to access data using WWW?
    a) HTTP b) HTML
    c) FTP d) SMTP
18. Which is not the programming language ?
    a) Pearl b) Python
    c) C^{+++} d) Basic
19. Which of the following is a interpreted programming language?
    a) Pearl b) C
    c) C^{++} d) Pascal

20. Which is a compiled programming language?

    a) C b) C++

    c) Pascal d) All of the above

21. Pearl is available for

    a) Windows b) LINUX

    c) Macintosh d) All of the above

22. Which of the following variable is not used in pearl ?

    a) Scalar b) Hashes

    c) Array d) Character

23. Which among the followings is not a gene finding tool?

    a) PHRAP b) FGENEH

    c) Net Gene d) GeneMark

24. DNA sequence data can be submitted to the ________ publicly accessible database

    a) Gene Bank at NCBI

    b) DNA Data Bank of Japan (DDBJ)

    c) European Bioinformatics Institutes (EBI)

    d) All of these

25. Comparative genomics is the comparing of genomes of different species which involve __________

    a) Sequence Similarity

    b) Location of genes

    c) Length and number of exons within genes

    d) All of these

26. Which among the following is the tool for peptide mass mapping and sequencing?

    a) DDBJ b) SEAQUEST

    c) SWISS-2DPAGE d) Peptide Search

27. Biological data base contains _____________.

    a) DNA b) Proteins

    c) Structures d) All of the above

28. NCBI is a ____________.
    a) Primary Database b) Secondary Database
    c) Composite Database d) Non of the above
29. SWISS- PROT is a database of__________.
    a) Nucleic Acid b) Structures
    c) Protein sequences d) None of the above
30. DDBJ is a repository of _____________.
    a) USA b) Europe
    c) India d) Japan
31. Which one is not a primary database?
    a) EMBL b) DDBJ
    c) OWL d) SWISS-PROT
32. Which one is not a secondary database?
    a) PROSITE b) CATH
    c) NCBI d) Pfam
33. Nucleic Acid database is abbreviated as __________.
    a) NAD b) NDB
    c) NADB d) None of the above
34. In sequence analysis we do not align ____________.
    a) Match characters b) Mismatch characters
    c) Two gaps or Blanks d) None of the above
35. In pair wise sequence alignment we compare ___________.
    a) More than two sequences b) Only two sequences
    c) Both A and B are correct d) None of the above
36. We can perform multiple sequence alignment for _________.
    a) Nucleotide sequences
    b) Protein Sequences
    c) Expressed Sequence Tags (ESTs)
    d) All of the above

Answer Key

1.	**b**	2.	**a**	3.	**d**	4.	**d**	5.	**c**	6.	**d**	7.	**d**	8.	**b**
9.	**c**	10.	**c**	11.	**d**	12.	**a**	13.	**b**	14.	**d**	15.	**b**	16.	**d**
17.	**a**	18.	**c**	19.	**a**	20.	**d**	21.	**d**	22.	**d**	23.	**a**	24.	**d**
25.	**d**	26.	**d**	27.	**d**	28.	**a**	29.	**c**	30.	**d**	31.	**c**	32.	**c**
33.	**b**	34.	**c**	35.	**b**	36.	**d**								

Fill in the Blanks

1. The application of genomic approaches and technologies to the identification of drug target is known as_______________.
2. 1 GB is equal to________________ bytes.
3. The concept of internet was given by _______________.
4. The full form of URL is ______________.
5. The first popular web browser was___________________.
6. BLAST stands for ______________________.
7. ___________ is the first Wi-Fi enabled city of India
8. Maximum number of Genome sequencing projects has been carried out at ________________.
9. Full form of BASIC is ________________.
10. 1 The term GENOMICS was given by ___________.
11. The DNA sequencing approaches had been evolved in year _________.
12. Frederick Sanger and his colleagues sequenced the genome of _________ in 1977 using dideoxy nucleotide chain termination method .
13. The Genome of x X174 _________bp nucleotides.
14. The complete set of m-RNA in an organism is called as _________________.

15. Entire protein content produced by a cell or organisms is called as ___________.

16. NCBI stands for __________________.

17. Paralogous sequences arise due to ____________.

18. Orthologous sequences arise due to ____________.

19. PAM stands for ________________.

20. BLOSUM stands for _______________.

21. BLAST stands for _________________________.

22. CLUSTALW program generally used for ______________ alignment.

23. UPGMA stands for ___________________.

24. PCA stand for ____________________.

25. _______________ is considered to be the father of Microarray Technology.

Answers of the Blanks

1. Pharmacoinformatics
2. 1073741824
3. J.C.R.Licklider
4. Uniform Resource Locator
5. Mosaic
6. Basic Local Alignment Search Tool
7. Mysore (Karnataka)
8. USA
9. Beginners all purpose Symbolic Instruction Code
10. 1 Thomas H. Roderick
11. 1997
12. x X174
13. 5386

14. Transcriptome
15. Proteome
16. National Centre for Biotechnology Information
17. Gene duplications
18. Speciation
19. Point Accepted Mutation
20. Block Substitution Matrix
21. Basic Local Alignment Search Tool
22. Multiple Sequence Alignment
23. Unweighted Pair group method with arithmetic mean.
24. Principal Component Analysis.
25. Mark Schean

Answer as True or False

1. International Rice Genome Project was initiated by USA.
2. India has sequenced a part of the Rice chromosome 11.
3. *Arabidopsis thaliana* is considered as the model organism.
4. Interchange of purines to pyrimidines is known as transition.
5. Inter change of purines to purines is known as transversion.
6. KEGG is the on line resources for information on molecular pathways.
7. PDB is the universal repository of protein structural database.
8. A change in DNA sequence at single residue is known as SNP.
9. 2D-PAGE is the technique for the separation of protein only according to its molecular weight.
10. Tandem repeats of nucleotides on genome are known as SSCP.
11. BLAST tool was developed by *Altschul et al.* in 1990.
12. PERL is the versatile scripting language used in Bioinformatics.
13. cDNA are used for genomic library construction.
14. Entrez is the on line data retrieving tool developed by the NCBI.

15. Branching graph used to represent the phylogenetic relationship is known as dendrogram.
16. Bioinformatics is the branch of information technology deals with storage and analysis of biological data.
17. SAGE is the method for the DNA sequencing.
18. X-ray crystallography is the technique for protein sequencing.
19. Hanikoff and Hanikoff in 1992 developed BLOSUM matrices.
20. Dayhoff and her associate developed PAM matrices.

Answer of the True or False

1. False
2. True
3. True
4. False
5. False
6. True
7. True
8. True
9. False
10. False
11. True
12. True
13. False
14. True
15. True
16. True
17. False
18. False
19. True
20. True

Match the Followings

Group A	Group B
1. Needleman-wunsch algorithm	A. Primer Designing Software
2. Smith-Waterman algorithm	B. Phylogenetic Analysis Software
3. PCR	C. Transcriptome study
4. Primer3	D. Global Sequence Alignment
5. NTSYS	E. Next Generation Sequencing
6. Pyrosequencing	F. Sulphur containing Amino Acid
7. Microarray	G. Aromatic Amino Acid
8. Methionine	H. MAPMAKER software
9. Phenylalanine	I. J.Craig venter
10. Unigene	J. Archive of Journal and Lterature
11. QTL	K. ClustalW
12. Celera Genomics	L. GeneBank
13. Multiple Sequence Alignment	M. EST database
14. PubMed central	N. Karry mullis
15. NCBI	O. Local Sequence Alignment

Answers of Match the Followings

Group A	Group B
1.	D
2.	O
3.	N
4.	A
5.	B
6.	E
7.	C
8.	F
9.	G
10.	M
11.	H
12.	I
13.	K
14.	J
15.	L

10

Sample Paper-I

1. They are bags of hydrolytic enzymes that bring about degradation of macromolecules
   a) Mitochondria b) Lysosomes
   c) Chloroplast d) Nucleus
2. What is the function of mitochondria?
   a) Generation of ATP b) To prepare foods
   c) In cell lyses d) None of the above
3. It is the mechanism by which cells internalize extracellular macromolecules
   a) Exocytosis b) Phagocytosis
   c) Endocytosis d) None of the above
4. Name the Sulfur containing amino acids.
   a) Valine and Glycin
   b) Phenylalanine and tyrosine.
   c) Histidine and proline
   d) Cysteine and methionine
5. Give the names of aromatic amino acids.
   a) Phenylalanine and tyrosine.
   b) Leucine and methionin
   c) Valine and Glycine
   d) Aspargin and glutamine
6. Give an example of an imino acid.
   a) Valine b) Histidine
   c) Proline d) Methionin

7. Benzene group is present in which amino acid?
   a) Histidin b) Glycin
   c) Phenyl alanine d) Prolin

8. The amino acid that cannot be synthesized in the body; and so, they are to be provided in the diet.
   a) Essential amino acids
   b) Non Essential amino acids
   c) Non necessary amino acids
   d) None of the above

9. How many amino acids are essential?
   a) 14 b) 12
   c) 10 d) 20

10. Which is an essential amino acid?
    a) phenyl alanine b) Arginine
    c) Serine d) proline

11. The pH at which the molecule carries no net charge is called
    a) Same pH b) Neutral pH
    c) Iso-electric point d) Neutral point

12. What are natural amino acids?
    a) D amino acids b) L amino acids
    c) Both A and B d) None of Above

13. Cupric ions in alkaline medium form a violet colour with peptide bond nitrogen.
    a) Xanthoproteic test b) Millon's test
    c) Molisch's test d) Biuret reaction

14. Will amino acids give a positive biuret test?
    a) No b) Yes
    c) Not predictable d) No Idea

15. Macromolecule made up by polymerisation of amino acids through peptide bonds
   a) Glycosides b) Cabohydrate
   c) Lipids d) Protein
16. How many peptide bonds are present in a tripeptide?
   a) 3 b) 4
   c) 2 d) 6
17. It denotes the number and sequence of amino acids in the protein.
   a) Primary structure
   b) Secondary structure
   c) Tertiary structure
   d) Quaternary structure
18. Sudden heritable changes in genetic makeup of individual called
   a) Recombination b) Evolution
   c) Replication d) Mutation
19. What is the function of oxido-reductases?
   a) Transfer of Hydrogen b) Transfer of H_2O
   c) Transfer of O_2 d) All of Above
20. What is the full form of NAD?
   a) Nicotinosine adenine dinucleotide
   b) Nicotinine adenine dinucleotide.
   c) Nicotinamide adenine dinucleotide
   d) Nicotinamide adenine diphosphate
21. That area (site) of the enzyme where catalysis occurs is referred to as
   a) Active site b) Action site
   c) Recognition site d) None of the above
22. Thermodynamically, the reaction in which energy is produced is classified?
   a) Endothermic reaction b) Exothermic reaction
   c) Iso therimc reaction d) None of the above

23. What is the immediate treatment for methanol poisoning?

a) NaOH b) Methanol

c) Acetone d) Ethanol

24. Enzymes whose concentration in a cell is independent of inducer are called

a) Constitutive enzymes b) Indusible enzymes

c) Both A and B d) None of the above

25. The term refers to the movement of charged particles through an electrolyte when subjected to an electric field

a) Sothern blotting b) Chromatography

c) Electroporation d) Electrophoresis

26. It is the ratio of the distance travelled by the substance (solute) to the distance travelled by the solvent.

a) Rf value b) Rt value

c) Rm value d) Rx value

27. Monosaccharides are combined together through

a) Phosphate bond b) Peptide bond

c) Glycosidic linkages d) None of the above

28. Name a few pentoses

a) Arabinose, Xylose, Ribose

b) Glucuse, fructose

c) Arabinose, robose

d) Galactose, xylose

29. Which isomer of carbohydrate is common in nature?

a) L variety of sugar b) D variety of sugars

c) Both A and B d) None of the above

30. Which is the most common monosaccharide in the body?

a) Glucose b) Starch

c) Sucrose d) Lactose

31. Which is the sugar found in milk?
   a) Maltose b) Lactose
   c) Fructose d) Sucrose
32. What is the reserve carbohydrate in plant kingdom?
   a) Cellulose b) Sucrose
   c) Glucose d) Starch
33. In this pathway, glucose is converted to pyruvate or lactate, along with production of a small quantity of energy
   a) Glycolysis b) Gluconeogenesis
   c) Glycogenolysis d) All of the above
34. In aerobic glycolysis, the net yield from one glucose molecule is how much?
   a) 12 ATP b) 2 ATP
   c) 8 ATP d) 38 ATP
35. During complete oxidation, what is the net yield of ATP from one glucose molecule?
   a) 8 ATP b) 12 ATP
   c) 2 ATP d) 38 ATP
36. How many ATPs are generated per one rotation of the citric acid cycle?
   a) 8 ATP b) 12 ATP
   c) 2 ATP d) 38 ATP
37. Pyruvate is converted to acetyl CoA by which enzyme?
   a) Pyruvate dehydrogenate
   b) Acetyl CoA synthetase
   c) Pyruvate Symthatase
   d) None of the above
38. What is the level of fasting blood sugar in a normal person?
   a) 120-150 mg/dl b) 40-70 mg/dl
   c) 70-110 mg/dl d) 150-210 mg/dl

39. Which one is the example of milk protein ?

a) Pepsin b) Trypsin

c) Casein d) Lectins

40. Where is insulin synthesised?

a) Pancreas b) Stomach

c) Kidney d) Heart

41. Which type of fatty acids is prevalent in human body?

a) Odd chain fatty acids

b) Even chain fatty acids

c) Both A and B

d) None of the above

42. How many carbon atoms are present in arachidonic acid?

a) 18 carbon b) 16 carbon

c) 22 carbon d) 20 carbon

43. What if full form of PUFA?

a) Poly Unused Fatty Acids

b) Poly Undigestible Fatty Acids

c) Poly Unsaturated Fatty Acids

d) Poly Unsaturated Free Fatty Acids

44. Which food stuffs contain cholesterol?

a) Non-vegetarian food

b) Vegetarian

c) Both A and B

d) No relation with food stuff

45. What is good cholesterol?

a) LDL cholesterol b) HDL cholesterol

c) Both A and B d) None of the above

46. Name polyunsaturated fatty acids
    a) Linoleic and linolenic acid
    b) Acetic acid and propionic acid
    c) Arachidic acid
    d) Palmitic acid
47. They act at one of the protein molecule, liberating amino acids sequentially, one at a time
    a) Exopeptidases b) Endopeptidases
    C Both A and B d) None of the above
48. Lysine is deficient in which food stuffs?
    a) Pulses b) Cereals
    c) Both A and B d) None of the above
49. Which amino acid will give rise to a vitamin?
    a) Aspargine b) Histidine
    c) Tryptophan d) Glutamine
50. How many ATPs are generated per one rotation of the citric acid cycle?
    a) 12 ATP b) 8 ATP
    c) 2 ATP d) 38 ATP
51. How many ATP are produced in the oxidation of one molecule of NADH?
    a) Two b) Three
    c) Four d) Eight
52. How many ATP are produced in the oxidation of one molecule of FADH?
    a) Two b) Four
    c) Eight d) Thirty eight
53. The antigen binding capacity of immunoglobulin resides at which region of immunoglobulin?
    a) Constant region b) Variable region
    c) Both A & B d) None of the above

54. How many molecules of oxygen can bind with one hemoglobin?

a) Four b) Three

c) Two d) One

55. Why carbon monoxide becomes a poison?

a) Hb has more affinity to carbon monoxide than oxygen

b) Hb has more affinity to carbon dioxide than oxygen

c) Hb has les affinity to carbon monoxide than oxygen

d) Hb has less affinity to carbon monoxide than oxygen

56. What is the pro-Vitamin for Vitamin A?

a) Beta carotene present in plants

b) Alpha carotene

c) Vitamin B

d) None of the above

57. Nyctalopia is due to the deficiency of which Vitamin?

a) Vitamin D b) Vitamin C

c) Vitamin B d) Vitamin A

58. What is the function of Vitamin E ?

a) Anti-oxidant b) Anti Ageing

c) Both A and B d) None of the above

59. Beberi is due to the deficiency of which Vitamin?

a) Thiamine b) Vitamin B6

c) Vitamin B12 d) Vitamin C

60. Pellagra is seen in the deficiency of which Vitamin?

a) Niacin b) Vitamin A

c) Vitamin B6 d) Both A & C

61. What is the precursor of niacin?

a) Glycin b) Valine

c) Tryptophan d) Phenyl allanine

62. Which is the Vitamin totally absent in plant sources?

a) Vitamin B_{12} b) Vitamin A

c) Vitamin C d) Vitamin B_6

63. Which is the trace element, deficient in milk?

a) Iron b) Mg

c) Mn d) Zn

64. What is the calorific value of carbohydrates?

a) Nine kilocalories per gram

b) Four kilocalories per gram

c) Two kilocalories per gram

d) One kilocalories per gram

65. What is the calorific value of fats?

a) Nine kilocalories per gram

b) Four kilocalories per gram

c) Two kilocalories per gram

d) One kilocalories per gram

66. When pH falls by 1 unit, what is the change in the hydrogen ion concentration?

a) Increases by 100 times b) Increases by 10 times

c) Decreases by 100 times d) Decreases by 10 times

67. What is a nucleotide?

a) Nitrogenous base + sugar

b) Nitrogenous base + phosphate

c) Nitrogenous base + sugar + phosphate

d) None of the above

68. Name the common purines

a) Adenine b) Cytosine

c) Uracil d) Thymine

69. Which nitrogenous base is absent in DNA?

a) Adenine
b) Guanine
c) Cytosine
d) Uracil

70. Which base is found exclusively in DNA and not in RNA?

a) Adenine
b) Guanine
c) Thymine
d) Cytosine

71. What is relationship between the A+T and G+C contains of DNA.

a) A+T = G+C
b) A+T > G+C
c) A+T < G+C
d) No Relation

72. What are the enzymes required for DNA replication?

a) DNA polymerase
b) Topo isomerase
c) DNA ligase
d) All of the above

73. Replication is in which direction?

a) 5' to 3'
b) 3' to 5'
c) Both directions
d) None of the above

74. Which enzymes protect cellular ageing?

a) DNA polymerase
b) RNA polymerase
c) Telomerase
d) Reverse transcriptase

75. What is transcription?

a) The process of making a complementary mRNA copy of DNA
b) The process of making a DNA copy of DNA
c) The process of protein synthesis from RNA
d) None of the above

76. What is the initiating codon for protein synthesis?

a) UAA
b) UAG
c) UGG
d) AUG

77. Which enzyme is required for PCR (Polymerase Chain Reaction)?

a) RNA polymerase
b) Reverse transcriptase
c) Taq polymerase
d) All of the above

78. What is the causative organism of AIDS?

a) Human amino deficiency virus
b) Acquire immune deficiency virus
c) HIS
d) Human immunodeficiency virus

79. Lactose is made up of

a) Glucose + Galactose
b) Glucose + Fructose
c) Glucose + Glucose
d) None of the above

80. Who first synthesized urea in laboratory?

a) Kuhne
b) Lavoisier
c) Neuberg
d) Wohler

81. Red colour of tomato is due to the presence of

a) Anthrocynin
b) Chlorophyll
c) Lycopene
d) Tomatin

82. The toxin presence in young sorghum seedling

a) Steroid
b) Saponin
c) Hordin
d) Dhurrin

83. The flavor in onion and garlic is due to the presence of

a) Allyl propide
b) Lycopene
c) Garlic
d) Allyl sulphide

84. The organ of plant that exhibit negative geotropism

a) Stem
b) Root
c) Both
d) None

85. The immediate precuasor of gibbrelline

a) Ethylene
b) Aspartic Acid
c) Acetic Acid
d) Kaurene

86. The mass of undifferentiated cell is called as

a) Callus b) Mass
c) Explants d) Suspension

87. O_2 of photosynthesis come from

a) CO_2 b) Plants
c) H_2O d) None

88. Embryo culture is helpful in

a) Recovery of distance hybrids
b) Propagation of orchids
c) Shortening of breeding cycle
d) All of the above

89. Cultivation of Apical Meristem as specially shoot Meristem is called

a) Embryo culture b) Pollen culture
c) Meristem culture d) Cell culture

90. Meristem culture is useful in

a) Vegetative propagation
b) Recovery of virus free stock
c) Germplasm conservation
d) All of the above

91. For obtaining haploid plants

a) Meristem culture b) Anther culture
c) Shoot tip culture d) None of above

92. 1 nm is equal to

a) 10^{-9} meter b) 10^{-9} cm
c) 10^{-9} um d) 100 A^0

93. In C_4 plants the initial acceptor of CO_2 is

a) Ribulose 1- 5 biphosphate
b) Phosphophenol puruvic acid
c) Both A and B
d) None of the above

94. Kreb cycle is also known as

a) Citric acid cycle
b) Tricarboxylic cycle
c) Both A and B
d) None of the above

95. Hormones that induce fruit ripening.

a) Ethylene
b) Cytokinines
c) Auxins
d) Gibberellins

96. The double helix structure of DNA was discovered by

a) Michaelis and Menten
b) Berzelius
c) Meselson and Stahl
d) Watson & Crick

97. The process of formation of complex substances from simple monomeric unit involving the energy is known as

a) Catabolism
b) Metabolism
c) Anabolism
d) All of the above

98. Who invented the PCR?

a) Kary mullis
b) Hargovind khurana
c) Arber
d) Kornberg

99. Name the trisaccharide

a) Raffinose
b) Stachyose
c) Both A and B
d) None of the above

100. Which is the most common gelling agent use in tissue culture

a) Agar Agar
b) Gum
c) Agarose
d) All of the ablove

Answer Key

1. **b**	2. **a**	3. **c**	4. **d**	5. **a**	6. **c**	7. **c**	8. **a**
9. **c**	10. **a**	11. **c**	12. **b**	13. **d**	14. **a**	15. **d**	16. **c**
17. **a**	18. **d**	19. **a**	20. **c**	21. **a**	22. **b**	23. **d**	24. **a**
25. **d**	26. **a**	27. **c**	28. **a**	29. **b**	30. **a**	31. **b**	32. **d**
33. **a**	34. **c**	35. **d**	36. **b**	37. **a**	38. **c**	39. **c**	40. **a**
41. **b**	42. **d**	43. **c**	44. **a**	45. **b**	46. **a**	47. **a**	48. **b**
49. **c**	50. **a**	51. **b**	52. **a**	53. **b**	54. **a**	55. **a**	56. **a**
57. **d**	58. **c**	59. **a**	60. **d**	61. **c**	62. **a**	63. **a**	64. **b**
65. **a**	66. **b**	67. **c**	68. **a**	69. **d**	70. **c**	71. **a**	72. **d**
73. **a**	74. **c**	75. **a**	76. **d**	77. **c**	78. **d**	79. **a**	80. **d**
81. **c**	82. **d**	83. **d**	84. **a**	85. **d**	86. **a**	87. **c**	88. **d**
89. **c**	90. **d**	91. **b**	92. **a**	93. **b**	94. **c**	95. **a**	96. **d**
97. **c**	98. **a**	99. **c**	100. **a**				